Praise for other books by M

FreeBSD Mastery: Storage Essentials

"If you're a FreeBSD (or Linux, or Unix) sysadmin, then you need this book; it has a *lot* of hard-won knowledge, and will save your butt more than you'll be comfortable admitting. If you've read anything else by Lucas, you also know we need him writing more books. Do the right thing and buy this now." – *Slashdot*

"There's plenty of coverage of GEOM, GELI, GDBE, and the other technologies specific to FreeBSD. I for one did not know how GEOM worked, with its consumer/producer model – and I imagine it's complex to dive into when you've got a broken machine next to you. If you are administering FreeBSD systems, especially ones that deal with dedicated storage, you will find this useful." — *DragonFlyBSD Digest*

Sudo Mastery

"It's awesome, it's Lucas, it's sudo. Buy it now." – *Slashdot*

"Michael W Lucas has always been one of my favorite authors because he brings exceptional narrative to information that has the potential to be rather boring. *Sudo Mastery* is no exception." – Chris Sanders, author of Practical Packet Analysis

Absolute OpenBSD, 2nd Edition

"Michael Lucas has done it again." – *cryptednets.org*

"After 13 years of using OpenBSD, I learned something new and useful!" – *Peter Hessler, OpenBSD Journal*

"This is truly an excellent book. It's full of essential material on OpenBSD presented with a sense of humor and an obvious deep knowledge of how this OS works. If you're coming to this book from a Unix background of any kind, you're going to find what you need to quickly become fluent in OpenBSD – both how it works and how to manage it with expertise. I doubt that a better book on OpenBSD could be written." — *Sandra Henry-Stocker, ITWorld.com*

"Do you need this book? If you use OpenBSD, and have not yet achieved guru status, yes, this book is just for you. Even gurus will find valuable things in this book that they did not know... But beyond the OpenBSD aspect, there are great sections on cross-platform applications like *sudo* that are almost enough on their own to justify getting this book. And there are several of those chapters. So: even if you don't use OpenBSD directly, would you like a quick reference on *sudo*, IPv6 networking, and NFS setup? Oh, and also *tftpd*, PXE, and diskless BSD systems? But wait, what if I told you these references came with a free book on OpenBSD installation and configuration?" – *Warren Block, wonkity.com*

"It quickly becomes clear that Michael actually uses OpenBSD and is not a hired gun with a set word count to satisfy... In short, this is not a drive-by book and you will not find any hand waving." – *Michael Dexter, callfortesting.org*

DNSSEC Mastery"

"Pick up this book if you want an easy way to dive into DNSSEC." — *psybermonkey.net*

SSH Mastery

"…one of those technical books that you wouldn't keep on your bookshelf. It's one of the books that will have its bindings bent, and many pages bookmarked sitting near the keyboard." — *Steven K Hicks, SKH:TEC*

"…SSH Mastery is a title that Unix users and system administrators like myself will want to keep within reach…" — *Peter Hansteen, author of The Book of PF*

"This stripping-down of the usual tech-book explanations gives it the immediacy of extended documentation on the Internet. Not the multipage how-to articles used as vehicles for advertising, but an in-depth presentation from someone who used OpenSSH to do a number of things, and paid attention while doing it." — *DragonFlyBSD Digest*

Network Flow Analysis

"Combining a great writing style with lots of technical info, this book provides a learning experience that's both fun and interesting. Not too many technical books can claim that." — *;login: Magazine, October 2010*

"The book is a comparatively quick read and will come in handy when troubleshooting and analyzing network problems." —*Dr. Dobbs*

"Network Flow Analysis is a pick for any library strong in network administration and data management. It's the first to show system administrators how to assess, analyze and debut a network using flow analysis, and comes from one of the best technical writers in the networking and security environments." — *Midwest Book Review*

Absolute FreeBSD, 2nd Edition

"I am happy to say that Michael Lucas is probably the best system administration author I've read. I am amazed that he can communicate top-notch content with a sense of humor, while not offending the reader or sounding stupid. When was the last time you could physically feel yourself getting smarter while reading a book? If you are a beginning to average FreeBSD user, Absolute FreeBSD 2nd Ed (AF2E) will deliver that sensation in spades. Even more advanced users will find plenty to enjoy." — *Richard Bejtlich, CSO, MANDIANT, and TaoSecurity blogger*

"Master practitioner Lucas organizes features and functions to make sense in the development environment, and so provides aid and comfort to new users, novices, and those with significant experience alike." — *SciTech Book News*

"...reads well as the author has a very conversational tone, while giving you more than enough information on the topic at hand. He drops in jokes and honest truths, as if you were talking to him in a bar." — *Technology and Me Blog*

Cisco Routers for the Desperate, 2nd Edition

"If only Cisco Routers for the Desperate had been on my bookshelf a few years ago! It would have definitely saved me many hours of searching for configuration help on my Cisco routers. . . . I would strongly recommend this book for both IT Professionals looking to get started with Cisco routers, as well as anyone who has to deal with a Cisco router from time to time but doesn't have the time or technological know-how to tackle a more in-depth book on the subject." — *Blogcritics Magazine*

"For me, reading this book was like having one of the guys in my company who lives and breathes Cisco sitting down with me for a day and explaining everything I need to know to handle problems or issues likely to come my way. There may be many additional things I could potentially learn about my Cisco switches, but likely few I'm likely to encounter in my environment." — *IT World*

"This really ought to be the book inside every Cisco Router box for the very slim chance things go goofy" — *MacCompanion*

Absolute OpenBSD

"My current favorite is Absolute OpenBSD: Unix for the Practical Paranoid by Michael W. Lucas from No Starch Press. Anyone should be able to read this book, download OpenBSD, and get it running as quickly as possible." — *Infoworld*

"I recommend Absolute OpenBSD to all programmers and administrators working with the OpenBSD operating system (OS), or considering it." — *UnixReview*

PGP & GPG

"...The World's first user-friendly book on email privacy...unless you're a cryptographer, or never use email, you should read this book." — *Len Sassaman, CodeCon Founder*

"An excellent book that shows the end-user in an easy to read and often entertaining style just about everything they need to know to effectively and properly use PGP and OpenPGP." — *Slashdot*

"PGP & GPG is another excellent book by Michael Lucas. I thoroughly enjoyed his other books due to their content and style. PGP & GPG continues in this fine tradition. If you are trying to learn how to use PGP or GPG, or at least want to ensure you are using them properly, read PGP & GPG." — *TaoSecurity*

Networking
for Systems
Administrators

Michael W Lucas

Tilted Windmill Press

For Liz

Brief Contents

Complete Contents

Acknowledgements

The people who most deserve thanks for this book are the folks who struggled through me learning networking as I stood between them and what they wanted to accomplish. Every one of you brought me some horrible issue that educated me even as you ranted and cried and begged for me to fix the problem. I learn slowly, and you suffered for it. Thank you. Fortunately, suffering builds character, so you got something out of it and I don't have to feel *too* bad.

This book had a crew of excellent technical reviewers. Some of them have an understanding of networking that crushes mine. Others knew nothing about networking, but were able to tell me when I confused them. Both are invaluable. They are, in alphabetical order: Alexiei Bottino, Donald Cooley, Fred Crowson, Michael Dexter, Dominik Douville-Bélanger, Edwin Groothuis, Josh Grosse, Bryan Irvine, Chris Josephes, Frank Moore, Kurt Mosiejczuk, Scott Murphy, Chris Parr, Martin Pugh, Mike O'Connor, A.J. Reese, Amanda Robinson, Jim Salter, Justin Sherrill, Carsten Strotmann, Grant Taylor, and Giovanni Torres. You all had excellent advice and lots of really good recommendations. Those recommendations would have made this book four times longer, but they really were excellent.

This book was made possible through hardware purchased from iX Systems (http://www.ixsystems.com). Well, not exactly *possible*. More like "a heck of a lot easier than trying to keep a maddening mishmash of recycled debris booting without bursting into great fountains of toxic flame."

And a special thanks to the people who've thrown a few bucks into my Tilted Windmill Press tip jar. You folks make writing for a living a lot more realistic.

Chapter 0: The Problem

Dear systems administrators: the firewall people don't want to talk to you, either.

It's nothing personal. We all share the goal of delivering service to users, but once you break that goal down into meaningful parts our teams completely diverge. Our tools differ. Our equipment differs. We even think differently. Sysadmins care about bytes, network administrators measure everything in bits. Network equipment might be built on computer hardware, but it's very specialized hardware that doesn't have any of the tools that systems administrators take for granted. Servers have network interfaces, but not nearly enough of them to do anything interesting.

Neither one understands how the other can possibly perform their job without the basic tools their platform offers.

Both roles require a high degree of specialization, especially in modern enterprises. The firewall administrator doesn't have time to dig into the specifics of the latest version of whatever operating system you're using. You don't have time to figure out why the newest version of the big firewall is mangling your carefully-crafted HTTP headers.

This is all complicated stuff. While I spend more time in systems administration than network engineering, I've filled both roles in the last twenty years. Each time I switch from one hat to the other I spend a few weeks catching up with the latest annoyances.

The end result? The network folks blame the servers. The server people blame the network. Often the blame gets personal. "It's the sysadmin's fault!" "If the firewall crew knew what they were doing, this wouldn't happen!" Meanwhile the helpdesk folks—correctly— blame everyone for not making customers stop whining. I've been in organizations where the only thing that prevented open warfare between IT teams was a shortage of sharp stabby objects.

Even in the best environments, differing expertise and priorities make both jobs more difficult than they have to be. Many organizations avoid this warfare by applying trouble tickets, workflow, and meetings. Lots and lots of brain-numbing meetings.

It doesn't have to be this way.

A systems administrator can't learn the ins and outs of each version of networking gear any more than a network administrator can learn the ins and out of the latest generation of your operating system. Neither one of you has the time to keep up with this constantly changing information on top of your own area of expertise.

A network administrator can—and should—learn the basics of how a server operates. Every network administrator should understand the basics of user access control and privileges, processes, services and daemons, basic installation and removal of software, and so on. But this information varies wildly between operating system platforms. Sometimes it's a language difference—Unix-like operating systems have daemons, while Microsoft systems have services. Sometimes even closely related operating systems have very different ways to handle similar tasks, such as the myriad ways of installing software on various Unix-like operating systems, or even on one operating system![1] The network administrator might learn the basics of the operating systems in your organization, but this knowledge won't carry forward to her next assignment.

Systems administrators can learn the basics of networking, however. And this knowledge will serve you no matter what

---

1   Solaris, I'm looking at you. Well, at your grave, but still…

organization you work with or what sort of network gear your organization uses. You don't need to know how to configure a router or a firewall or any other network device—they're all ephemeral anyway.

But basic TCP/IP knowledge endures. While people add new protocols all the time, these are incremental changes and easily mastered. It's *much* easier to teach a systems administrator the basics of networking than it is to teach a network administrator the basics of systems administration, and that knowledge will last your entire career.

Understanding the network saves you time. You won't wonder if a network change has been made—you'll check it yourself. You won't call to see if a problem is inside your network—you'll look and find out. You'll quickly determine if problems exist on your systems, on your network, or outside your network.

Most network administrators quickly learn which systems administrators understand basic networking and which don't. When I'm a network administrator I'm happy to work with the sysadmins that don't ask me if I've opened that firewall port or if there's a problem between here and our office in Farawayistan. Being asked "When will the link to Farawayistan be fixed?" might be harder to answer, but it does save a loop in the conversation.

If I'm a network administrator with a whole stack of issues to resolve, but I know that you speak from evidence when you say "This traffic isn't reaching my server," I'll address your problem before everyone else's. There's a really good chance that I can fix your problem quickly because you provide me with actual information. If my phone is ringing like mad and everything seems to have collapsed, resolving your problem might solve problems for a whole bunch of other people.

Make yourself the most valued member of your systems administration team. Take a couple hours to read this book, learn a little networking, and become a bridge to other critical IT groups.

We'll start by discussing network principles, and then go into detail on how to view or use those principles on multiple operating systems. This book covers Windows, Linux (CentOS and Debian), and BSD platforms, but the principles and tools run on just about any modern networked operating system, including portable devices like phones and tablets.

Who Should Read This Book?

Every sysadmin, database admin, web admin, developer, and computing professional should understand the basic principles of networking. This book grounds you in modern TCP/IP without demanding a month's dedicated study. Understanding the network will empower you to identify the real source of problems, solve your own problems more quickly, and make better requests of your team members.

This book is also for network administrators who need to educate others in their team about the essentials of networking. After a few years, a network administrator's understanding of TCP/IP turns into an interconnected morass of window scaling and sequence numbers and malformed packets. Someone asks what a port is, and moments later you're explaining SYN floods and the questioner has learned the vital lesson of "never ask the network administrator *anything*." (This trait isn't exclusive to network administrators—it's endemic in the IT industry. Ask a database administrator to explain databases sometime.[2]) That stuff is all vital to a network administrator's job, but

---

2   I'm not responsible for your sanity, or loss thereof, if you actually do ask this.

the average user doesn't need to understand it. You can use this book to explain only what the average sysadmin absolutely must know about TCP/IP.

Server versus Network Device

By *server* I mean a computer, running an operating system, whose main task is providing services to other servers or users, rather than supporting the network. A *sysadmin* is someone responsible for managing such devices.

Some network administrators build routers, firewalls, proxy servers, intrusion detection devices, and more out of carefully selected server hardware. When this book says *server*, I'm explicitly excluding such custom-built devices. Elsewhere I say that a server should never do X, but if you've built a device whose purpose is doing exactly that, it's an exception.

When I mention a *router* or *proxy server* or any number of other network devices, I mean a device that fills that role. It doesn't matter if it's a black box solution or something built out of commodity hardware. The *network administrator* is the person who manages that equipment.

A Note to Network Administrators

Some readers are network administrators, wondering how the heck I'm going to teach networking in a few pages. Let me answer your questions before you ask them.

I don't dive deep into network protocols. My explanations might not be totally accurate for all situations and all environments. Every protocol has its edges, and I'm not trying to cover them all. The goal of this book is not to make sysadmins networking professionals, but to equip them with the skills they need to take better care of themselves and disturb you less frequently.

I skip a lot of old knowledge. The Ethernet chapter covers switches and not hubs. You won't encounter a hub by accident these days. They are specialized devices only deployed in specific cases.

I don't cover many traditional networking topics, because they're not absolutely essential. SNMP, or the Simple Network Management Protocol, is one example. I could fill a book this size discussing SNMP. I do discuss how ICMP is built on top of IP, when the specification wedges it in this misshapen role between the network and transport layers. But someone who's unclear on TCP versus UDP doesn't need to go into SNMP right now, or Netflow, or VLAN propagation, or any of the innumerable protocols used to manage and diagnose networks. Understanding SNMP won't change someone's relationship with the network team the way understanding TCP/IP will.

Always remember that I'm talking to non-network administrators. I'm not going to tell sysadmins that they can, say, use a /112 IPv6 subnet, because not everybody's equipment can do that. I play the heavy here by spelling out the rules: you get to swoop in and tell your people that yes, your network can break certain rules because you are *so* totally amazing. I'm also consciously and deliberately glossing over some protocol details, so you can explain them and make your sysadmins think you're terribly smart. You can thank me later.

Network Tools

If you look around you'll find innumerable server-side tools for analyzing the network. Many of these tools work only on very specific operating systems or have limited utility. I will cover tools that work across both Microsoft and Unix platforms, and have been widely ported to less common operating systems like VMS.

Yes, some operating systems have their own network analysis tools, but that knowledge isn't portable throughout your career. If a piece of software is Windows-only, or Oracle-only, or Debian-only, I won't cover it. Once you understand the cross-platform tools, you can quickly apply that knowledge to platform-specific tools.

The Windows network debugging tools are all designed for the command line. I recommend you not use the traditional Windows command window CMD.EXE. Try Microsoft's PowerShell or Cygwin's mintty. Any version of either one should suffice, although newer versions are probably less buggy and more secure. Neither one will sink its fangs into you, and after about three minutes of acclimation you'll be much happier. I normally use Cygwin and mintty, but the software behaves the same under PowerShell.

You can combine all of these tools with your usual system utilities like tail(1), Wordpad, or whatever your preferred platform offers.

Here's the main tools I cover.

ifconfig, route and ipconfig

A host's network configuration includes its IP addresses and gateway. On Unix, use the `route` and `ifconfig` commands to view the system's network configuration. Windows systems put all of these in the `ifconfig` command. While different operating systems have different versions of these commands, you can sort out the information you need from any of them.

Microsoft has added networking functions to PowerShell. While I do recommend learning and understanding PowerShell, recommending you start with PowerShell would be like shoving you in the deep end of the ocean and telling you to swim back to Switzerland. If networking becomes a big part of your work, get comfortable with PowerShell's networking commands.

Similarly, some Linux variants have started to move away from `ifconfig`, but it will be available and supported for some time to come, and it's the command most Unixes use for network configuration. I'll give some basics on Linux's replacement commands, ip and ethtool. If you're a specialist in a Unix-like operating system that's invented their own thing, you need to understand the replacement. The ifconfig command will get you started, though. A minimal install of CentOS doesn't include ifconfig, but it's in the net-tools package.

grep and findstr

Many network-related commands produce far more output than you want to read. The grep (Unix) and findstr (Windows) commands let you search for a specific string within a pile of output. I'll demonstrate these commands by example.

I do encourage Windows sysadmins to install one of the many versions of grep on your systems, as it's far more flexible than findstr. You must install a few other network troubleshooting programs anyway, why not one more? Once you learn a little grep, you'll wonder how you ever managed a system without it.

netstat

The netstat command displays a system's established network connections, what connections the system can receive, and network statistics. Some operating systems, like Solaris, use netstat to show the routing table. Many operating systems offer most of their visibility into the network through netstat.

lsof

The Unix command lsof lets you see what processes open which files. Unix treats network connections much like files, so I'll demonstrate using lsof to peek at their innards.

route

The `route` command both displays where the system sends traffic, and gives you the ability to change how the system delivers traffic.

tcpdump and Wireshark

The `tcpdump` command displays traffic to and from a server, even when the server rejects that traffic. `tcpdump` is the fastest way to view network activity. For more complicated analysis, you'll probably want to use Wireshark.

Many operating systems include their own traffic sniffing program, such as `snoop` on Solaris and Microsoft's Network Monitor and Message Analyzer. There's nothing wrong with these tools, but expertise in them doesn't carry over into other operating systems. Most of them use syntax copied from `tcpdump`, however. An understanding of `tcpdump` makes using platform-specific tools much easier.

Not all operating systems ship with `tcpdump`, and Wireshark is always an add-on package. You might need to install it from your operating system's packaging system. I'll discuss installation more in detail in Chapter 9.

netcat

The `netcat` program lets you listen to the network on a specific port, and lets you send arbitrary network traffic. It's a great way to verify that the network will let you send and receive traffic without configuring a specific daemon or service for that purpose.

Not all operating systems include `netcat` by default. Chapter 10 covers installing `netcat`.

traceroute

A network is a collection of linked devices that pass traffic between hosts. Most networks can use a variety of routes between hosts. The `traceroute` program (`tracert` in Windows) shows you the route that traffic takes and where these links break.

Not all operating systems ship with `traceroute`. You might need to install it from your operating system's packaging system. See Chapter 12 for details.

host and nslookup

The `host` (Unix) and `nslookup` (Windows) commands let you peek at the Domain Name Service, which maps host names to IP addresses. Configuring DNS fills books, but viewing DNS data offers insight into many problems.

While I recommend `nslookup` on Windows, on Unix use `host` rather than `nslookup`. Microsoft has specifically extended their version of `nslookup` to support modern DNS. Unix `nslookup` has been deprecated, abandoned, and then resurrected and repaired. Which version does your Unix install include? Most often, a bad one. Don't risk it. Use `host` instead, or a more advanced tool like `dig` or `drill`.

Book Contents

I've divided this book into two sections.

Chapters 1-6 teach the parts of network technology that systems administrators really should know. You'll learn how to investigate how your server is attached to the network and basic connectivity issues.

Chapter 1, *Network Layers*, covers the network's logical units and how they fit together.

Chapter 2, *Ethernet*, discusses the most commonly used datalink layer.

Chapter 3, *IPv4*, teaches you about the version of Internet Protocol used for the last three decades or so.

Chapter 4, *IPv6*, goes on to the next generation Internet Protocol that we'll all be using at some future date.

Chapter 5, *TCP/IP*, explores the protocol stack that dominates the Internet.

Chapter 6, *Viewing Network Connections*, teaches you how to view network activity on your own system and which programs are attached to the network.

Chapters 7-12 take you from passively looking at the network to actively probing your equipment and examining the results. What can speak to what? What traffic is reaching your server, and is your server answering?

Chapter 7, *Network Testing Basics*, offers guidance on how to use network testing tools without causing conflict with the rest of your organization.

Chapter 8, *the Domain Name System*, discusses the DNS, how it impacts systems administration, and how to investigate name service issues.

Chapter 9, *Packet Sniffing*, covers observing network traffic. You can watch connections as they enter and leave the system.

Chapter 10, *Creating Traffic*, shows how to use `netcat` to generate and receive arbitrary traffic to test connectivity.

Chapter 11, *Server Packet Filtering*, gives some advice and perspective on deploying packet filtering on your own machines, whether they're on private networks or the public Internet.

Chapter 12, *Tracing Problems*, discusses the misunderstood `traceroute` tool and how to diagnose problems on the wider network.

With this much knowledge, you'll be able to get yourself into all sorts of trouble!

Chapter 1: Network Layers

The network contains physical wires or radio waves, interconnection devices like switches, logical protocols like TCP/IP, user-visible web pages and emails, and more. In one sense these are all stirred together into a gumbo of bits, but really they're divided into several logical layers for convenience and simplicity. Each layer handles a very specific task and usually interacts only with the layers immediately above and below it.

System administrators often use the phrases *network layers* or *application layers* in a completely different sense. Your complicated web application might have a database layer, a storage layer, and a web server layer. This is a completely valid use of the word "layer" and perfectly appropriate in your context, but be aware that the network folks mean something utterly different.

Layers are critical in troubleshooting. When a layer breaks, it takes all the layers above with it. Diagnosing a network problem requires first identifying the lowest layer that has a problem. When you fix that bottom layer, the rest of the network should come back up—unless you have multiple simultaneous problems, of course. Saying "a web site is down" is roughly equivalent to calling up a skyscraper manager and saying "I can't reach the penthouse." If the second floor is on fire, time spent troubleshooting the penthouse locks is wasted.

Layers let you more precisely express where an issue is. A trouble ticket that says "my server is down" might get a reply of "no it's not." Both sides might be strictly accurate, but nothing gets resolved. A trouble ticket that says "here's the diagnostic output that shows a layer 3 problem, but layer 2 works fine" will get a much better response.

The layered network model is often called a *network stack* or the *TCP/IP stack*.

Common Network Layers

Textbooks often talk about the Open Systems Interconnect (OSI) seven-layer model, but that's more academic than real-world. The TCP/IP model is a much better fit for modern networks, but it lacks some of the detail of the OSI model. This book presents a slightly modified TCP/IP model, because I discuss the physical wire separately from the datalink protocol on top of it.

To understand the modern Internet-attached network you need only five layers: physical, datalink, network, transport, and application. Network layers are often referred to by number.

Layer 1: Physical

Networks must travel over something. If you can trip over it, snag it, break the stupid tab off the plastic connector at its end, or broadcast static over it, it's the physical layer. Many of us call the physical layer the *wire*, although it can be radio waves or coaxial cable or any number of things other than a typical Ethernet wire. If your wire meets the standard defined for that type of physical layer, you have a network. If not, your network won't run.

Most servers connect to a network via an Ethernet cable, usually over a cat5 or cat6 cable but sometimes over optical fiber. Even if the server uses a non-Ethernet protocol such as Asynchronous Transfer Mode (ATM) or Token Ring or FDDI or whatever, it probably uses cat5, cat6, or optical fiber. Try very, very hard to not connect servers to the local network via wireless. (No, harder than that.) Wireless is very prone to datalink layer errors and interference, and can be overloaded by forces beyond your control or even your awareness.

The physical layer traditionally has no intelligence. The datalink layer determines how it's used.

Layer 2: Datalink

The datalink layer transforms the network's upper layers into the signals transmitted over the wire. Most environments use Ethernet as the datalink layer. A single lump of datalink data is called a *frame*.

If you're running IPv4 (Chapter 3), the datalink layer includes Media Access Control (MAC) addresses and the Address Resolution Protocol (ARP). IPv6 (Chapter 4) uses MAC addresses and Neighbor Discovery (ND). If you're having trouble exchanging data with your local network, go to those chapters and check for ARP or ND issues.

Layer 3: Network

Isn't the whole thing a network? Yes, but the network *layer* maps connectivity between hosts. This is where the system answers questions like "How do I get to this other host? *Can* I get to this other host?" The network layer provides a consistent interface to network programs, so they can use the network over any physical and datalink layers. A single chunk of network data is called a *packet*.

The Internet uses the Internet Protocol, or IP. That's the IP in TCP/IP. All versions of IP give each host one or more unique IP addresses, so that any other host on the network can find it. Network address translation (NAT) screws around with the "unique address" rule, but somewhere on your network or on your provider's network you have a globally unique IP address.

You'll see two different versions of IP: version 4 (Chapter 3) and version 6 (Chapter 4).

Layer 4: Transport

The data you care about flows at the transport layer. The lower layers of the stack exist to support the transport layer. A piece of transport layer data is a *segment*. The three most common transport layer protocols are the Internet Control Message Protocol (ICMP), the Transmission Control Protocol (TCP), and the User Datagram Protocol (UDP).

ICMP handles low-level connectivity messages between hosts. Every host that implements IP must also support ICMP. While ping requests are the most commonly known type of ICMP traffic, many core Internet functions rely on ICMP. If a datalink-layer message (a frame) is too large, the complaint passes over ICMP. ICMP is where hosts respond to ping requests and tell traffic to go around the other way. Unilaterally blocking all ICMP is a good way to break applications.[3] Most of the time, ICMP runs silently in the background.

UDP and TCP carry application data between hosts. They are so common that the suite of Internet protocols is usually called TCP/IP. (UDP/TCP/IP is too unwieldy.) UDP, or User Datagram Protocol, offers the minimal services needed to transmit data over the network. While people joke that the U in UDP stands for *unreliable*, it's meant for applications where reliability is handled in the application rather than the network. TCP, or Transmission Control Protocol, includes error-checking, congestion control, and retransmission of lost data, but it lacks the flexibility and simplicity of UDP.

The transport layer includes many protocols beyond these three, as we'll discuss in Chapter 5.

Most applications speak either TCP or UDP. Some use both.

---

3   Yes, some network administrators unconditionally block all ICMP from entering or leaving their network. They are almost always wrong. At least you know what you're dealing with, though.

Higher Layers

According to the OSI model the next layers are *session*, *presentation*, and *application*. The session layer handles opening, using, and closing transport layer connections. The presentation layer lets programs exchange data with one another, and the application layer is the actual protocol spoken over these connections.

In practice, however, these layers aren't deployed so frequently or so cleanly. Certain applications use them. Others just pour you straight into the program's functions. An application vendor might have designed their software with three layers, but perhaps not.

The TCP/IP model calls everything above the transport layer the *application* layer. This includes protocols like HTTP, SMTP, LDAP, and everything else, including most of what you manage. I find this a more realistic description of how our networked systems behave.

Layering in Practice

Let's look at a very simple, stripped-down network request. You open your web browser and call up a web page. The browser spins a moment and shows you the result. What's really going on here? Your browser takes your request, gets the IP address for the site, and asks the operating system for a connection to that IP address on TCP port 80.

The transport layer in the operating system kernel takes the request and slices it into chunks small enough to fit inside TCP segments (536 bytes or smaller). It hands these segments down to the network layer.

The network layer only cares about where that segment needs to go. If the network layer knows how to reach the destination address it wraps each segment with IP information to create a packet and hands the packet off to the datalink layer.

The datalink layer doesn't know about IP addresses, let alone web browsers. It only knows how to launch packets at a particular MAC address at the other end of a piece of wire. The datalink layer adds information for the physical protocol to the packet, creating a frame, and sends it across the wire.

The wire carries the frame to the destination, where the target computer strips off the layers, reassembles the request, and hands it up to the web server. The web server processes the request and returns a response, which takes the same journey back. That's an awful lot of work just for a 404 error.

Between the two computers you might have switches, or routers, or all kinds of equipment. The packet might traverse many different datalink layers. One of the jobs of a router is to strip a frame's datalink information for one physical layer and add the datalink layer for a new physical layer before sending on the packet.

Taken all together, between your application's web server layer and your database layer you'll find a physical layer, a datalink layer, a network layer, and a transport layer. What sort of layer you're talking about becomes clear from context—once you know the layers exists!

Layers and Troubleshooting

Understanding network layers is vital to successful network troubleshooting.

Why are network layers important? If a lower layer fails, all the layers above it also fail. Troubleshooting the upper layer might indicate an error, but won't expose the actual problem. A command like `ping` offers insight into the network layer, while `netcat` tests the transport layer. If these commands fail, try `arp` to check the datalink layer, and look at the interface link light to see if the cable's plugged in.

IT professionals react more strongly to specific information than generalities. Calling up the network administrator and saying "I can't get on the network" is a generality. This might be a network problem, a server problem, something another sysadmin did, or something the network administrator broke. The statement "The server has a link light on this connection, but I'm not getting an ARP reply from the gateway" immediately narrows the problem scope to something the network administrator is almost certainly involved in—especially if this machine worked yesterday! It still might be your issue, but every network administrator will agree that further diagnosis requires her involvement.

We'll go deep into troubleshooting each layer in later chapters, but let's take a quick look to get started. Table 1 shows the various layers and suggested troubleshooting tools.

Table 1: Network Layers & Troubleshooting Tools

layer	name	suggested tools
1	physical	link light, ipconfig/ifconfig, cable replacement
2	datalink	arp, ND, tcpdump
3	network	ping, traceroute
4	transport	netstat, netcat, tcpdump
5+	yours	logs, debuggers

Let's talk briefly about why and how each tool applies to each layer. Further chapters have more details.

Physical Troubleshooting

The physical layer is simultaneously the simplest layer and the most vexing. Cables don't come with a light that turns red when they fail, and they don't send log messages or SNMP traps to your monitoring server. But if your Ethernet cable is miswired or you've pinched it until it shorts out, if someone staples through your coax, or someone

19

mounts their wireless router right next to your wireless base station, the physical layer breaks and your network either performs badly or totally fails. It's hard to say which is worse. The physical layer offers two troubleshooting interfaces: interface commands and link lights.

Most operating systems have a way to see if the physical layer is working. On Windows systems, the Network and Sharing Center displays all interfaces. The words "unplugged" and "disconnected" are really good hints that the physical layer isn't healthy.

Most Unix systems use `ifconfig` to display the link status. On a BSD system you can check `ifconfig`'s `media` line to see an interface's negotiated speed and duplex. On a Linux box, run `ethtool` and give the interface name as an argument.

If you're physically near the machine, a link light on the network card indicates that the card can see the other end. The link light doesn't mean that it's successfully negotiated a network connection, merely that it can see something alive on the other end of the wire.

If you don't have a link light, but the cable looks good and the interface isn't disabled in the operating system, ask the network administrator if this connection's switch port is turned off. Some switches disable ports when they see specific errors from the other end, and the switch might have disabled your server to protect the rest of the network.

You might also have a speed and duplex mismatch. Check the negotiated values on the host and the switch.

Theoretically, a network cable lasts forever. A good cable won't break unless abused, but a cable of borderline quality might work fine until someone sneezes near it. While you can and should test cables before deploying them, some cables that pass tests are more resilient than others. In practice, if you suddenly experience weird, intermittent issues and your troubleshooting tools don't expose a root cause, replace the cable and see what happens.

The bad cable might not be the one attached to your server. If your connection goes to a patch panel, there's probably another patch panel somewhere else with a cable going to a switch. While most (not all) network administrators are fine with a sysadmin replacing the cable between their server and the patch panel, don't try to go anywhere past your own patch panel. Many patch panels are nonintuitively wired. The nice friendly numbers on one end might not correspond to the numbers on the other end, and the cable that obviously goes to your gear quite possibly doesn't. Leave them alone.

Bad network cables have this weird ability to crawl out of trash cans and back into a server. *Always* chop a failed cable in half before discarding it, preferably in such a way that you have loose wires dangling everywhere so that nobody tries putting a new end on it.[4]

Datalink Troubleshooting

For your common Ethernet network, the `arp` command is your friend. This lists the other Ethernet addresses that your operating system sees on the network. Chapter 2 discusses `arp`.

The ARP table only shows Ethernet addresses that should appear on your configured IP address range. If you suspect an IP misconfiguration, use `tcpdump` (Chapter 9) to see what traffic the host receives from the network.

In addition to ARP-style errors, you might get Ethernet framing errors. All operating systems have a way to view such datalink layer

---

4   I'd recommend a stake through the heart, but Ethernet cables hide their hearts in remote, isolated places.

errors, but sometimes you must dig for them. We'll look at those in Chapter 2.

Network Troubleshooting

When the network layer fails, your host cannot deliver packets to hosts beyond the local subnet. Investigate network issues with tools like `ping` (Chapter 2) and `traceroute` (Chapter 12).

Transport Troubleshooting

At the transport layer, things get complicated. Use `netstat` to view established connections. Use `netcat` (Chapter 10) to see if you can transmit data to another host. (Many people will suggest using `telnet` to test data transmission, but Chapter 10 also explains why that's not a great idea.) Try `tcpdump` (Chapter 9) to see if data arrives at your server and verify your host is actually sending data.

Now let's spend some quantity time with Ethernet.

Chapter 2: Ethernet

Ethernet is the standard local area network protocol, with an overwhelming share of the market. While you might encounter protocols like ATM or token ring, Ethernet pretty much obliterated its competitors before the turn of the millennium.

Ethernet is a broadcast protocol. Every frame transmitted can go to any other host on that section of the network. Either your network core, the server's network card, or the card's device driver separates out data intended for your system from the data meant for other systems. A section of Ethernet where all the hosts can communicate directly with each other, without involving a router, is called a *broadcast domain*, a *segment*, or a *local area network* (LAN). Which is the proper term? It depends on your equipment vendor. Most network engineers have a preferred term, but will understand when you use any of them. I use the term "broadcast domain" through this book. I recommend avoiding the term "segment" as many other protocols, such as TCP and UDP, also have segments.

Each host is wired to a port on an Ethernet *switch*. You probably have a small switch on your home network, but large switches can have hundreds or thousands of ports.

Every device on an Ethernet needs a unique identifier, called a *MAC address* or *Ethernet address*. A MAC address is 48 bits long, usually written as six pairs of colon-separated hexadecimal numbers (such as 52:54:00:3b:2b:25). Windows systems use a dash instead of a colon, so you get values like 9C-B6-54-1C-D4-E3. Network gear sometimes prints MAC addresses as three groups of four hexadecimal characters each, separated by periods. This address identifies your machine on the local network. The first six numbers of the MAC address identifies the Ethernet card manufacturer.

While Ethernet is a broadcast medium, and every host on an Ethernet can spray traffic across the whole local network, switches reduce the amount of traffic sent to each host by filtering each port by MAC address. If the switch knows that the MAC address 52:54:00:3b:2b:25 is connected to switch port 87, it sends traffic for that MAC address exclusively to that port.

On common Intel-style hardware, both 32-bit and 64-bit, the MAC address is assigned to the Ethernet card.[5] On higher-end hardware, such as Oracle's SPARC servers, the MAC address is a property of the server.

Speed and Duplex

Ethernet comes in a variety of speeds. You might see gear that does 10 megabits per second (Mbps), but that equipment is almost gone today. Most desktop network interfaces do at least 100Mbps or 1 gigabit per second (Gbps). Many servers do 10Gbs. Kit for 40Gbs and 100Gbs is starting to appear.

Duplex refers to how each end handles transmitting and receiving data. An interface running at half duplex can either receive or transmit data at any instance, but not both. A full duplex connection can simultaneously send and receive.

---

5   Some Ethernet cards let you change the MAC address in software. This is a great way to attract your network administrator's attention, unfavorably.

For a connection to work well, both sides must agree on speed and duplex. If your server insists on speaking 1Gbs, but the switch insists on 100Mbps, the connection will not work. If they disagree on duplex, the connection might appear to work but will lose frames under load.

All modern equipment supports full duplex connections. A connection running at half duplex should be a hint that something is not right and that part of this link is defective.

Modern equipment *autonegotiates* connection speed and duplex, agreeing on the fastest settings both sides support. Some older equipment autonegotiates poorly, requiring you to hard-code the speed and duplex on the server and the switch. Setting speed and duplex varies widely between operating systems, so I recommend you check your manual for details. If autonegotiation fails, Ethernet cards automatically set themselves to 10Mbs, half duplex.

Gigabit and faster Ethernet connections negotiate much more than speed and duplex, and autonegotiation is a mandatory part of the protocol. While some network cards let the sysadmin hard-code gigabit speed and full duplex, this is mostly a facade to make the sysadmin feel like he's done something. Gigabit Ethernet always autonegotiates the connection, but if you hard-code it to gigabit speed it negotiates like a jerk, and insists it will only accept a gigabit connection.

Early versions of autonegotiation, more than ten years ago, were flaky and caused enough trouble that many system and network administrators disabled them and hard-coded all network settings. Today, autonegotiation works much better. I recommend autonegotiating unless you have specific reasons not to, such as a hardware bug.

If one side of a connection is set to autonegotiate, and the other has hard-coded settings, you will probably get a duplex mismatch.

Cisco's document "Troubleshooting Cisco Catalyst Switches to NIC Compatibility Issues," available at a search engine near you, has a great table spelling out the various failure modes of autonegotiation and hard-coded speed and duplex, but they all come down to: don't do that. Set both sides identically, even if the setting is autonegotiation.

An Ethernet's speed is not how fast the card can pass traffic. It's how fast the datalink protocol can pass traffic between the network card and the switch, provided that all of the hardware involved can keep up. The protocol speed effectively says both sides speak the same language, but not how fast each side can actually exchange traffic. Gigabit Ethernet first appeared on hardware incapable of sending even 100Mbps, just so that vendors could advertise the new feature.

Even today, very few gigabit network cards actually exchange data at gigabit speed. If a server's maximum network throughput seems too low, the motherboard might not be able to push as much traffic as the card's marketing indicates. Or you might have a lousy card—I've owned more than one "gigabit card" that could handle less than a hundred megabits. Some cards interrupt too frequently when they get under load, dragging the whole system to a crawl. Some vendors claim that they actually push the stated amount of traffic, but if you read the fine print you'll see that they used carefully designed traffic to reach that throughput. If a network card speaks gigabit, it's called a gigabit card even if it can only push half a megabit.

Fragments and MTU

TCP/IP wraps one layer inside another until you create a frame and throw it across the network. Every datalink type, from Ethernet to T1 to fiber OC48, has a maximum frame size. What happens when a packet is too large for the datalink layer's frame? An application might build a 65,507-byte packet, but that's way too large to fit in a 1500-byte

T1 frame or even a 9000-byte Ethernet jumbo frame. It's too big for any datalink layer, on any medium.

If a layer receives a chunk of data too large for it, it *fragments* that data into pieces that it can manage. When the data reaches the destination, the destination system reassembles those fragments into a complete unit. Fragmentation increases load on both the server and the client.

Most systems set a maximum transmission unit (MTU), the largest size that can fit through the datalink layer. The upper layers of the stack respect this MTU, eliminating obvious problems. Older Ethernet has an MTU of 1500 bytes. Some 100Mbs Ethernet, and all gigabit and faster Ethernet, support 9000-byte "jumbo" frames. Many gigabit environments don't choose to enable jumbo frames, however. The MTU should be set per-network.

I've been involved in more than one organization that manually set an MTU smaller than the default on all of their equipment, usually because of a specific business partner. Network hardware, server operating systems, and applications are designed for standard MTU sizes, and reducing the MTU beneath the maximum increases system load and might break applications, either obviously or subtly. Reducing MTU size below the standard can even break web browsing, especially if ICMP is also blocked. (ICMP is used to exchange MTU errors along a connection path.) It's far, far better to replace the hardware demanding a reduced MTU size, but if you're a small company and your biggest customer the multinational conglomerate tells you to make this change or stop doing business with them, you don't have much choice.

Never set a small MTU globally—you'll confuse your other equipment and annoy other business partners. Dedicate systems to that business partner, on a separate network, and only use that MTU for those systems, or set an MTU for only that partner's IP addresses.

The process to change MTU size is entirely operating system dependent, but your time is better spent pushing back against the requirement than looking it up.

Occasionally you'll need to change the MTU size on home equipment, notably gear behind certain consumer DSL links. This equipment is usually smart enough to permit the ICMP messages needed to negotiate the smaller MTU size. I usually recommend getting a better ISP.

How do you change the MTU? Sadly, every operating system has its own methods. Windows requires Registry changes, while every Unix-like variant has unique commands. You'll need to check your operating system manual.

Ethernet Wires

Most organization Ethernets run over physical wire. Ethernet can work over radio waves, but that has a maximum limit on the amount of traffic the whole network can put through it. You can observe this in a crowded coffee shop, and it would be worse in a fully wireless office. One limit on a host's network connection is the type of cable it's connected with.

Ethernet cable is ranked by category (or *cat*) number. Generally speaking, higher numbers are better. Category 5, "cat5" cable, is the usual lowest common denominator these days. It has a maximum throughput of 100Mbs. A cat5e cable can handle gigabit speeds. Datacenters might use cat6 cable, which can handle 10Gbps. If you're involved in the initial wiring of a new facility, you might consider cat7 cable, which can handle 40Gbs and is expected to replace HDMI cables before long.[6]

---

6   I expect, though, that you'll price cat7 and go with the cheaper cat6 instead. That's how the buildings wired with cat3 got that way, after all.

I know of some office buildings still wired with cat3 cable, rated at a maximum of 10Mbs. If you get that connection, cry. Then deploy carrier pigeons to enhance your throughput.

Testing Ethernet: ping

A "ping" is a very simple request transmitted to another system, basically saying "Hello? Are you there?" It's somewhat sonar-like, hence the name. You don't learn anything about the services the host supports. All Unix-like and Windows systems include `ping`. The day you start your first IT job, someone always tells you to ping hosts to see if they're live. That's not exactly what `ping` does, but it's useful for poking at your network.

The `ping` command needs one argument, the hostname or IP address you want to provoke a response from. Here I ping one of my test hosts from a Windows box. Windows sends four pings. Unix will ping until you tell it to stop. (If you want Windows ping to run until you tell it to stop, add the `-t` flag.) Hit CTRL-C to interrupt the ping.

```
> ping 203.0.113.50

Pinging 203.0.113.50 with 32 bytes of data:
Reply from 203.0.113.50: bytes=32 time=6ms TTL=64
Reply from 203.0.113.50: bytes=32 time=5ms TTL=64
Reply from 203.0.113.50: bytes=32 time=1ms TTL=64
Reply from 203.0.113.50: bytes=32 time=1ms TTL=64

Ping statistics for 203.0.113.50:
    Packets: Sent = 4, Received = 4, Lost = 0 (0% loss),
Approximate round trip times in milli-seconds:
    Minimum = 1ms, Maximum = 6ms, Average = 3ms
```

A successful ping will tell you how quickly each response came back from the target host. At the end, you'll get some statistics on how many responses you got and how quickly.

Here I'm trying to hit the host 203.0.113.205, again from a Windows box.

```
> ping 203.0.113.205
Pinging 203.0.113.205 with 32 bytes of data:
Reply from 203.0.113.57: Destination host unreachable.
Reply from 203.0.113.57: Destination host unreachable.
Reply from 203.0.113.57: Destination host unreachable.
Reply from 203.0.113.57: Destination host unreachable.

Ping statistics for 203.0.113.205:
    Packets: Sent = 4, Received = 4, Lost = 0 (0% loss),
```

So, this host isn't on the network... or is it?

The ping test tells you that you didn't get an answer from this host. It doesn't mean that the host isn't on the network. Let's dive into ARP and see what exactly happened here...

The Address Resolution Protocol

The *Address Resolution Protocol*, or *ARP*, maps Ethernet addresses to IPv4 addresses and back. ARP is the glue that attaches the network layer to the datalink layer.

A host that needs to transmit data to another host on the local Ethernet first broadcasts an Ethernet request asking "Which MAC address is responsible for this IP address?" These broadcasts go to all hosts attached to that Ethernet network. (That's where the term *broadcast domain* comes from, actually.)

A host that receives a request for an IP it owns jumps up, waves its hand, and shouts "Me! Me! I have that address, at MAC address such-and-such." When the original host gets this response, it adds the IP and MAC address to its ARP table. The original host can then send the destination host traffic.

The ARP Cache

When a host maps a MAC address to an IP address, it caches that information in the ARP table for a few minutes. Once the cache entry expires, it re-queries the network via ARP.

If an IP address' MAC address changes, hosts on the local network cannot reach it until their ARP caches expire. The operating system might realize that a MAC address is no longer correct and do a new ARP query, but any existing connections will hang for a moment. Most hosts only change their MAC address when you replace the network card, so this isn't a common issue unless you're being clever.

Some clever "live failover" protocols work by sharing a MAC address and an IP address between two hosts. When one host fails, the other host claims the MAC and IP address and continues providing the service. A common cause of failover failures is a slightly different MAC address on each host. The better failover implementations send an unrequested *gratuitous ARP* message to announce the new MAC address for an IP address.

Viewing the ARP Cache

Use the `arp -a` command to view a host's ARP table on both Windows and Unix systems. While the output differs between operating systems, they all contain the same basic information. Here I show the ARP table from a Windows system.

```
> arp -a
Interface: 203.0.113.57 --- 0xa
Internet Address        Physical Address        Type
203.0.113.1             d4-ca-6d-1a-dc-68       dynamic
203.0.113.54            b8-e9-37-2a-05-30       dynamic
203.0.113.55            b8-e9-37-1a-73-1e       dynamic
...
```

This system sees many hosts on the local Ethernet. You can assume that the local network is up and working.

A Unix system's ARP table contains more information, such as this FreeBSD machine.

```
# arp -a
? (203.0.113.57) at a4:db:30:33:2d:6c on em0 expires in
   1194 seconds [ethernet]
storm.blackhelicopters.org (203.0.113.50) at
   00:25:90:db:d5:94 on em0 permanent [ethernet]
? (203.0.113.1) at d4:ca:6d:1a:dc:68 on em0 expires in
   1183 seconds [ethernet]
```

This host is on the same network as our Windows host, so it can see the same MAC addresses. The only host on both lists is 203.0.113.1, however. This system has communicated with different hosts than the Windows box, so its ARP cache differs.

By default, Unix systems shows hostnames in ARP table entries. If the server can't get a name for the system, you'll see a question mark. This machine can't get hostnames for 203.0.113.57 or 203.0.113.1. To list the ARP cache contents without hostnames, add the −n flag.

The arp command, like just about everything else, uses the system name service (Chapter 8) to get names from IP addresses. If your name service runs slowly, arp hangs while trying to get those hostnames. This isn't very noticeable for one or two missing names, but if name services have failed your arp command might hang for several minutes. If this happens, interrupt the command with CTRL-C and run it again with the −n flag.

Most Unix systems also show the cache time for each entry. The entry for 203.0.113.57 expires in 1194 seconds, or about 20 minutes.

Note that the entry for 203.0.113.50 has no cache time. That's the IP address for the local host. Many Unix systems hard-code the MAC address for itself in the ARP table and label it "permanent."

Missing ARP

If a host doesn't have an ARP entry, your host either hasn't communicated with that host before, or the target host's ARP cache entry has expired. If you want to reach a host, see if you can ping it.

If the remote host doesn't answer pings, you can't assume that the host is unreachable. All you know from the ping test is that this host isn't responding to a layer 3 (network) request. It tells you nothing about the datalink or physical layers. You cannot check a remote server's physical layer from your machine, but you can check the datalink layer for hosts on your local network. Even if a host doesn't answer pings, it will answer the ARP request for that IP address. Did a host respond that it was responsible for this address?

While you can dump the entire ARP table, it's easier to request only the address you're looking for. On Windows, use `arp -a` and add the desired IP address.

```
> arp -a 203.0.113.205
```

On Unix systems, use the `arp` command and the IP, without the `-a`, like so.

```
# arp 203.0.113.205
```

In this case, the problem system has an ARP table entry.

```
? (203.0.113.205) at 00:ac:29:41:7d:90 on em0 expires in
  1141 seconds [ethernet]
```

It won't ping, but it has ARP? What's going on?

Maybe the system owner configured this machine to ignore ping requests. Maybe it's running in single user or recovery mode and doesn't have enough of a TCP/IP stack to respond. It's possible that your network administrator filters ping from the local network, but I've never seen that on an enterprise network except when someone screwed up.

If you're getting ARP from a system but cannot ping it, talk to the owner of the remote system before calling the network administrator.

If the ARP table shows no entry for an address, or the address is listed as "incomplete" or "missing," the datalink layer between the two hosts is broken. If you have connectivity to the rest of your local network, the host you're trying to reach is off-line. It might be either a system or network issue, but if this is the only problem host on the local network I'd ask the system owner first.

Empty ARP

If your system's ARP table is empty, or the only entry is the local host, try to connect to a few hosts on the local network. Ping the default gateway or a couple servers you know are local. These connection attempts should populate the system's ARP table.

If the ARP table is empty after trying to connect to a few local hosts, your system is not attached to the network. Verify the physical layer and your IP address configuration, then consult with the network team. You might try `tcpdump` (Chapter 9) to gather information before making that call, but you need the network folks to fix this.

Neighbor Discovery

Neighbor discovery (ND) is the IPv6 datalink protocol, replacing the Address Resolution Protocol used in IPv4 Ethernet. Neighbor discovery is supposed to work on all datalink protocols, not just Ethernet, but Ethernet is still the most common.

Neighbor discovery is extremely similar to ARP. The IP addresses are larger, and the state table has a few more entries. The ND designers tried to learn a few lessons from decades of experience with ARP. But in short, ND maps MAC addresses to IPv6 addresses. Neighbor requests are broadcast across the local network, and an individual host responds. Responses are cached in a table until they expire.

Unlike ARP, where entries are either present or missing, neighbor cache entries can have a few different states. *Reachable* addresses are currently live on the network. *Stale* addresses were live, but have since expired from the cache. *Permanent* addresses are either local on the machine, or special-purpose addresses that are always present. *Failed* addresses are neighbors the host has looked for but not found. There are a few more states that exist very briefly, but these are the ones you're likely to encounter.

Using neighbor discovery, again, varies widely between operating systems.

Windows ND

Viewing the neighbor discovery cache with Windows requires using `netsh`. While `netsh` is a very powerful tool, it's overkill for most beginners. The `netsh interface ipv6 show neighbors` command displays all IPv6 neighbors.

```
> netsh interface ipv6 show neighbors
...
Internet Address                     Physical Address    Type
------------------------             ------------------  ----------
2001:db8::1                          d4-ca-6d-1a-dc-68   Reachable
fe80::24b3:1094:9f53:c2e8 38-60-77-eb-b2-2d   Reachable
fe80::3060:21b4:1fef:1e0  74-de-2b-f6-79-e9   Reachable
fe80::bd42:8975:8156:c112 9c-b6-54-1c-d4-e3   Stale
fe80::d6ca:6dff:fe1a:dc68 d4-ca-6d-1a-dc-68   Stale (Router)
ff02::1                              33-33-00-00-00-01   Permanent
ff02::2                              33-33-00-00-00-02   Permanent
ff02::c                              33-33-00-00-00-0c   Permanent
...
```

Each IPv6 host this machine has communicated with appears in this list.

Unix ND

Each Unix variant has its own way to show IPv6 neighbors, most often with a unique command created just for the purpose. Solaris added displaying neighbors to the `netstat` command (`netstat -pn -f inet6`). Linux put it in the `ip` command (`ip -6 neighbor show`). BSD has the `ndp` command. Here's an IPv6 neighbors table from a CentOS machine.

```
# ip -6 neigh show
2001:db8::1 dev eth0 lladdr d4:ca:6d:1a:dc:68 router STALE
2001:db8::fecc:82fd dev eth0 lladdr 00:0c:29:cc:82:fd REACHABLE
2001:db8::99 dev eth0 FAILED
...
```

This host has tried to reach the host 2001:db8::99, but can't get a neighboring MAC address for it. The possible causes are identical to a missing ARP entry.

VLANs: One Cable, Multiple LANs

A local area network, or LAN, is an Ethernet broadcast domain. All the hosts on the LAN can see each other. But sometimes you need a special-purpose host on multiple LANs. The classic example is a firewall, which must see both the inside and the outside of an organization's network, but other systems can have similar needs.

The hard way to give a network visibility into multiple network segments is to give it multiple network interfaces. This requires spending money and possibly overprovisioning the server hardware. Most servers won't saturate the network cards they have, and adding more interfaces that they won't fill is less than optimal—not to mention the extra cables, switch ports, and other breakable tidbits. Your server might come with four gigabit ports on the motherboard, but if you won't ever saturate any of them, why hook them all up?

Sometimes you need separate cables for very specific security reasons. If you're in that type of environment, your security policy will say so. Or perhaps you actually need a huge amount of throughput. Your central backup server probably needs dedicated network connections.

If you don't need all that throughput, though, that's where a virtual LAN comes in handy.

Virtual LANs

A *virtual LAN*, or VLAN, is an extra tag on Ethernet frames indicating that they belong on a different LAN than the default. Ethernet frames that arrive at your network card without this tag belong in the default LAN, while frames carrying this extra tag are saying "I belong in this other LAN." These tags let you put multiple VLANs on a single physical wire.

Each VLAN is identified by a number from 1 to 4096. Your organization might have, say, VLAN 2 on the public Internet, VLAN 3 on the database tier, VLAN 4 on the fourth floor offices, and so on. The network team manages these assignments.

Operating systems can use virtual interfaces or sub-interfaces (the language varies by operating system) to handle VLANs. Each virtual interface has its own IP configuration. You might see an interface like eth0:1 on Linux, vlan0 on FreeBSD, or the arbitrary names Windows permits.

You cannot just make up a VLAN number and assume it'll work. The network team configures VLANs on the switches and assigns VLAN numbers. For a VLAN to function, the switch port your hosts connect to needs a VLAN configuration. Some switches auto-configure requested VLANs, while others require manual intervention.

Company security policy plays into how VLANs are arranged on your network. If you get clever and assign your own VLAN numbers to your servers and discover that they work, you're requesting the network team to a) come up with a better security policy, and b) slap you. If you need a VLAN, talk to the network team and get a number properly assigned.

You'll sometimes see VLANs described as 802.1Q, which is the exact VLAN standard that won this particular protocol war.

VLAN Terminology

The most confusing part of virtual LANs? The terminology. Different vendors have decided to use the same words to mean different things. The most problematic words are *trunk* and *tag*. Let's talk about trunks first.

According to one group of network equipment vendors, a *network trunk* combines multiple physical layers into one datalink layer. Your server gets two network cables, and you configure the server to group them together into one connection. This creates redundancy, so that a failure of one switch or one cable or one network card doesn't disconnect the server from the network. These kinds of trunks are very useful and popular.

Many other network vendors have defined a *network trunk* as one network cable that carries multiple VLANs. These kinds of trunks are also very useful and popular, but have no relationship whatsoever to the first vendors' use of the word.

Which group is right? Neither. Nobody owns the word *trunk*.

Similarly, some vendors use the word VLAN. Others talk about *tagging* or *VLAN tagging*. To create a VLAN, devices add a tag to an Ethernet frame. It's all the same thing.

Most network administrators use the language of their preferred vendor. If your company only uses network gear from company X, it almost certainly uses that company's terminology. Those of us who have been around for a long time either adopt our organization's language or, worse, use all of these terms interchangeably. If I'm your network admin, I might tell you that I've configured a trunk to your server. Or that I'm sending you some tagged VLANs. Or that I've configured a trunk on your trunk, at which point you're allowed to proceed directly to hard liquor.

If you're in doubt, ask your network administrator if this is the trunk with tagged VLANs or the trunk with multiple cables. Ignore the flinch, she can't help it.

Datalink Errors

The datalink layer can go bad without completely failing. Switch ports and cards can drop frames. Pinched cables can intermittently short out. A switch that has run fine for years can pick up one speck of dust too many. And when it comes to wireless, you'll get datalink errors any time someone with fillings walks through the room. You don't need to know the specifics of each error, but the common ones are *frame errors*, *drops*, *overruns*, and *collisions*. These errors reduce performance, but don't necessarily bring the link down. How can you see these problems, other than general "network slowness?"

Each operating system has its own method of displaying datalink errors.

Windows

If your host has only one Ethernet interface, use `netstat -e` to view Ethernet statistics. You'll see the number of bytes sent and received, as well as Discards and Errors.

```
> netstat -e
Interface Statistics

                         Received        Sent
Bytes                  3404421907  4214918690
Unicast packets         278970297   540725881
Non-unicast packets       1311625      280863
Discards                        0           0
Errors                          0           5
Unknown protocols               0
```

The Discards and Errors should always be zero in an ideal world, but a small number is probably okay.

Some versions of Windows break out netstat -e output by network interface. Others show the total number of errors, but not which interface has them.

If you suspect errors on a system with multiple network interfaces, and netstat doesn't show you which, you'll need to check each interface. Microsoft operating systems do not show Ethernet errors in the GUI by default, and don't officially support displaying them. Enabling display requires an undocumented registry change.
You can find registry files that implement this for you, but here's how you can do it yourself. Start regedit and browse to HKEY_ LOCAL_MACHINE\SYSTEM\CurrentControlSet\Control\ Network\Connections. Create the key StatMon under that key. In StatMon, create a REG_DWORD called ShowLanErrors. Set ShowLanErrors to 1. Reboot.

When you check a network interface's Status window, look in the Activity section. You'll see a line for Errors near the bottom.

Again, Microsoft does not officially support viewing datalink errors. They can change this registry key at any time. If you have trouble, check the various Microsoft chat sites and technical support.

It might just be easiest to call the network administrator and ask her if she's seeing any errors on your server's switch ports.

Unix

Use `netstat -i` to view datalink statistics, including errors. You'll see the numbers of frames that each interface has received and transmitted, as well as the number of errors on each. Every Unix-like operating system displays interface errors in its own format.

Some Unix systems also display datalink errors in `ifconfig` output.

Current or Old Errors?

The error counts on both Unix and Windows systems are totals since the system booted. If you see an error count, that doesn't mean that the system is currently taking errors. The server might have experienced datalink errors during boot, or during Ethernet autonegotiation, or when someone tugged a cable during a maintenance window, and has run clean ever since. When you see errors on an interface, determine if they're increasing or constant.

Some Unix `netstat` implementations have a `-w` flag that updates the output every few seconds.

If you've changed the Windows Registry to display errors, Windows will increment the display in real time. Hang out and watch the Status window.

Otherwise, on Windows and Unix alike, use `netstat`. Run it once. Wait a few seconds and rerun it. Compare the second results to the first. If the error count increases, you have a problem right now. If the error count is constant, the interface has stopped taking errors.

Note the wall clock time when you observe the errors, and how far apart you run the `netstat` command. Your network administrator might need the time and the error rate per second to troubleshoot.

Configuring Ethernet

Most of the time, you won't need to configure anything on an Ethernet card. On those occasions that you need to manually set the MTU size or change some other setting because your card is being stupid, you'll need to check your operating system specific documentation. Linux uses `ethtool`, while BSD uses `ifconfig`. Some systems have a configuration programs just for wireless Ethernet. I can't help you sort out your operating system's tools, but understanding what you're trying to achieve should make using the tools easier.

Now that you've got a handle on the datalink layer, let's go upstairs to the network. Layer 3, here we come!

Chapter 3: IPv4

The Internet Protocol, or IP, is the glue that binds the Internet together. IP version 4 has been the standard for the last three decades. If you want to do real work on the Internet you must have a basic understanding of IPv4.

Hosts meant for end users, like desktops, laptops, and tablets, normally get their configuration via the Dynamic Host Configuration Protocol (DHCP). Why wouldn't you do the same for servers and let the network administrator figure it all out? You can. Some cloud solutions rely on this. But even if you configure everything dynamically, understanding basic TCP/IP lets you troubleshoot connectivity issues.

To connect a host to a network it needs a valid IP address and a subnet mask. If it needs to communicate with hosts beyond the local network, it needs a default gateway. Knowing the addresses of your DNS servers is a definite plus.

IPv4 Addresses

An IPv4 address is a 32-bit number assigned to a specific network device, globally unique in your network. Some IP addresses are almost permanent, such as those assigned to the root DNS servers. The addresses used by desktops and mobile clients change as they move around the network or reboot. Server addresses can change, but those changes require coordination with other services.

Rather than a single large number, IP addresses are usually expressed as four eight-bit decimal numbers, such as 203.0.113.1. This "dotted quad" notation is easier to use and remember than 110010110 00000000111000100000001, or even 3,405,803,777.

A block of IP addresses is called a *network* or *subnet*. Your organization's Internet Service Provider (ISP) allocates a subnet to your organization. Your network administrator probably further divides that subnet among your organization. She probably also uses subnets designated for private use, such as any IP beginning with 10.

Strictly speaking, all the IP addresses on the Internet are one network. Every smaller allocation is a subnet, or a subnet of a subnet. The words "network" and "subnet" are often used in a context-dependent manner. An ISP issues your organization a network, which your network administrator divides into subnets—but the ISP's network administrator says he issued you a subnet of his network. (Again, the word *network* is badly overused. Do not confuse an IP subnet with the Ethernet broadcast domain or the generic term for layer 3 of the network stack.) If you split your slice of cake in two, you still have a slice of cake—it's just a smaller slice.

Hosts can only communicate directly with hosts on the same IP subnet. To communicate with hosts on a different network, they must go through a router—even if they're on the same Ethernet.

IP addresses are not free—they're a tightly managed scarce resource, and most companies must pay for them. An organization that wants more globally unique IPv4 addresses must carefully document its need and purchase them. Even then, your ISP might not have additional IP addresses available.

Also, most organizations do not own their own IP addresses. If your organization changes ISPs, they must return all of their IP addresses to their old ISP and get new ones from the new ISP.

Hopefully the network team verified that the new ISP had IP addresses available before agreeing to the move.

Each subnet contains a number of addresses equal to a power of 2. A subnet might contain, say, 8, 16, or 128 addresses, but not 22. 22 is not a power of 2. You can't chop a network of 256 IP addresses into 25 blocks of 10 addresses and one of 6—none of these are powers of 2. Subnets must *always* conform to the math. If an ISP gives you addresses that don't fit this pattern, you're sharing a network with someone else.

Netmasks and Network Size

Network subnets are the most math-heavy part of this book. It boils down to "the IP address and subnet mask assigned by your network administrator are sacred. Follow them with total obedience." If you want to know the details, read on.

A *netmask* indicates the size of a subnet—or, if you prefer, the size of a subnet dictates its netmask. Like an IP address, a netmask is a 32-bit number usually expressed as four decimal numbers, often called a *dotted quad*. Unlike an IP, a netmask is defined by its length in bits. The common 255.255.255.0 netmask is 24 bits long. A 24-bit netmask has the first 24 bits set to 1 and the remaining bits set to 0.

What does "length in bits" mean? A netmask is the number of fixed bits in the local network. For a 24-bit netmask, the first 24 bits in the IP address block cannot be changed. You've seen IP address ranges like 192.0.2.1-192.0.2.254. This looks like a classic "class C," 24-bit, or 255.255.255.0 network.[7] Hosts on the network can use any value between 1 and 254 for the last number, but if they change any of the

7   The classful network system was obsoleted in 1995, but even today some new books refer to it. Avoiding classful network language will get you brownie points with those snooty network engineers.

earlier numbers they lose access to other hosts on that network. A /25 network has 25 fixed bits, a /26 network 26 fixed bits. Here's a /26 in binary notation.

```
11111111111111111111111111000000
```

The first three groups of eight are binary 11111111, which is 255 in decimal. The last block is 11000000, which is 192. Put these together and you have a netmask of 255.255.255.192.

Netmasks are easy in binary. Most people don't think in binary, but after working with netmasks for a while you'll recognize legitimate decimal values. Some operating systems might display netmasks in hexadecimal, but they display lots of other things in hex, so you're probably okay with that.

If you don't want to do the math, many web sites offer subnet calculators. Table 2 in the next section includes a table of valid netmasks for small networks.

How does the netmask dictate the size of your network? If your address has 26 fixed bits, you can change (32-26=) 6 bits. 2^6=64, so your network has 64 IP addresses.

When combined with an IP address, a netmask is usually represented by a slash (/) and its bit length. That is, the IP 192.0.2.1 with a 24-bit netmask is written as 192.0.2.1/24. This is called *CIDR* (Classless Inter-Domain Routing) notation.

When IPv4 first came out, networks were split on boundaries of multiples of 8 bits. This is the "classful" system you'll see referenced in obsolete documentation. That's why you often see netmasks like 255.255.255.0, for a block of 256 IP addresses. But other netmasks are not only usable, they're common today. No organization gets a block of 256 public IP addresses without very specific circumstances.[8]

---

8   Or *very* special video footage.

Valid Netmasks

To make things a little easier, here's a table of netmasks longer than /24.

Table 2: Valid Netmasks

Slash	Decimal Mask	Available IPs
/24	255.255.255.0	256
/25	255.255.255.128	128
/26	255.255.255.192	64
/27	255.255.255.224	32
/28	255.255.255.240	16
/29	255.255.255.248	8
/30	255.255.255.252	4
/31	255.255.255.254	2

Not all of the available addresses are usable, however.

Unusable IPv4 Addresses

On a traditional network, the first and last IP addresses in a subnet are unusable for protocol design reasons. The bottom number is the network address, the top is the broadcast address. If you have the 203.0.113.0/24 network, the addresses 203.0.113.0 and 203.0.113.255 are unusable. There's nothing magic about the .0 and .255 numbers, they're only used in this case because that's the size of the network. On the 192.0.2.128/26 network, the addresses 192.0.2.128 and 192.0.2.191 are the top and bottom addresses, and hence unusable.

Some newer IP stacks allow using these unusable addresses. The problem isn't assigning these addresses to one of these new devices, however—it's what happens when an old device tries to communicate with the new device. Will your printer have a nervous breakdown when it gets a request from 203.0.113.0? Eventually this old gear will disappear, but for today hesitate to use top and bottom addresses.

Routers & the Default Gateway

A *router* is a device that sends traffic from one IP subnet to another. It might also convert one physical layer to another. A typical home cable modem is a router, connecting your home Ethernet to the cable company's coax or fiber. Routers can connect to multiple subnets, and can make intelligent routing decisions based on their information about the surrounding network.

If a host needs to get to a system that's not on the local network, it sends the packets to the *default gateway*. That's generally the router on the local network.

Traditionally, the router is either the first or last usable address in a subnet. It doesn't have to be, and don't be surprised if it isn't, but it is common practice.

The default router on an IPv4 network needs an IPv4 address. The default router on an IPv6 router needs an IPv6 address. These addresses might be on the same device, or not.

Some multi-tier networks have multiple routers in certain broadcast domains. Normally the main router sends an *ICMP redirect* message when the client tries to reach a host behind a secondary router, telling the client to go to the secondary router for that host. The client automatically sends all traffic for that destination address to the proper router.

Sometimes ICMP redirects don't work and you must configure static routes on your hosts. This is often because the network administrator has filtered ICMP redirects in compliance with the "all ICMP is dangerous and must be stopped" myth. Sometimes it's because the network team is stuck with some old gear that really needs to suffer a reciprocating saw-related accident. (Help them out if you can.) Some operating systems just don't like ICMP redirects, and they'll need static routes.

Or maybe you just have gremlins. It happens.

Servers should never need to run dynamic routing protocols like OSPF, EIGRP, RIP, BGP, and so on. I'd explain what they are, except that all a sysadmin needs to know is "Run away. Run away *now*." If you're curious about dynamic routing and want to play with it, do it on your own test network. Adding dynamic routing to a network someone else manages is a great way to ruin everyone's day.

Netmasks versus LANs and Gateways

More than one organization cursed with unexpected success discovers that they've outgrown their IP subnets and need more addresses in parts of the network. Maybe the dev team decided that they'd only ever need five database servers, so the network administrator allocated a block of eight IP addresses for that part of the network. Then the company has a sudden runaway hit, and they need twenty database servers *yesterday*.

The network administrator probably can't increase the subnet size, as that would drag in addresses used elsewhere. Instead, she adds a second IP subnet to the Ethernet broadcast domain. If the hosts in each IP subnet don't need to communicate with each other, there's no problem.

But then you put, say, a file backup and tape server on one of these subnets and have all of the servers on that broadcast domain back up their files to it. The backup runs far more slowly than you expect. Why?

Remember, hosts can only communicate directly with hosts on the same IP subnet. If a host is on a different IP subnet, it sends all traffic through the router. It doesn't matter if the two servers are on the same physical Ethernet; if they're on different IP subnets, all traffic goes through the router. IP knows nothing about Ethernet.

I've also seen people assign IP addresses outside the IP subnet, and then be surprised that they don't work. Assume that you have a server with the IP address 192.0.2.2/26. This is a block of 64 IP addresses. It can communicate directly with the IP addresses 192.0.2.1 through 192.0.2.63, and it sends all external traffic through the default gateway at 192.0.2.1.

Put a second host on the same Ethernet. Give it an IP of 192.0.2.100 and a netmask of /24. The subnet on the second host includes 192.0.2.2, so the second host will try to reach 192.0.2.2 directly. The first server knows that 192.0.2.100 is on a different subnet, as it's outside of its allocated range. The first server sends all responses to the second server through the router. The result is asymmetric traffic flow and poor or nonexistent connectivity.

Do not confuse "sharing an Ethernet with another host" and "able to directly connect to that host via IP!" These are different things.

Viewing IP Configuration

To see a host's IP configuration on Windows, use the `ifconfig` command. On Unix, use `ifconfig` and `route`.

When you can't get on the network, check the host's IP configuration. Verify the IP addresses. See if you can ping the gateway, or get ARP from it. If you can hit your gateway, ping your DNS servers and do DNS lookups (Chapter 8).

ipconfig

On Windows, run `ipconfig` to show the host's network state.

```
> ipconfig.exe

Windows IP Configuration

Ethernet adapter Local Area Connection:
   Connection-specific DNS Suffix : mwlucas.org
   Link-local IPv6 Address . . . . .:
                        fe80::cc81:b32f:b8a8:a569%10
   IPv4 Address. . . . . . . . . .: 203.0.113.57
   Subnet Mask . . . . . . . . . .: 255.255.255.0
   Default Gateway . . . . . . . .: 203.0.113.1
...
```

The `ipconfig` command shows every network interface, including ones you never knew existed, like disabled tunnels and software-specific interfaces. The network interfaces we care about right now are the Ethernet interfaces. This host has one Ethernet interface. You see the IPv4 address and subnet mask in dotted-quad notation, as well as the default gateway.

Windows shows much more information about a host's network interfaces if you add the `/all` flag to `ipconfig`. I've trimmed the output below to exclude information irrelevant to this section, such as IPv6 and DNS.

```
> ipconfig.exe /all

Windows IP Configuration
Ethernet adapter Local Area Connection:

   Description . . . .: Realtek PCIe GBE
   Physical Address. .: 9C-B6-54-1C-D4-E3
   DHCP Enabled. . . .: Yes
   IPv4 Address. . . .: 203.0.113.72
   Subnet Mask . . . .: 255.255.255.0
   Default Gateway . .: 203.0.113.1
   DHCP Server . . . .: 203.0.113.1
   DNS Servers . . . .: 8.8.8.8
```

We see the network card make and model, which is vital if you're researching possible performance problems with your hardware. The physical address is the MAC address for this network card. This host was configured via DHCP. Finally we get the IP addresses for the DHCP and DNS servers.

ifconfig and route

On Unix hosts, use ifconfig to view all network interfaces. On some operating systems, such as OpenIndiana and certain Linuxes, you must add -a to show all interfaces. (If your Linux system doesn't have ifconfig, use ip address show instead.) While Unix systems arrange their information differently, they all contain the same basic results. Here's the result from a Debian system.

```
# ifconfig -a
eth0 Link encap:Ethernet  HWaddr 00:0c:29:04:23:4c
     inet addr:203.0.113.206  Bcast:203.0.113.255  Mask:255.255.255.0
     inet6 addr: fe80::20c:29ff:fe04:234c/64 Scope:Link
     UP BROADCAST RUNNING MULTICAST  MTU:1500  Metric:1
     RX packets:10055 errors:0 dropped:1203 overruns:0 frame:0
     TX packets:114 errors:0 dropped:0 overruns:0 carrier:0
     collisions:0 txqueuelen:1000
RX bytes:928059 (906.3 KiB)  TX bytes:13832 (13.5 KiB)
lo   Link encap:Local Loopback
     inet addr:127.0.0.1  Mask:255.0.0.0
     inet6 addr: ::1/128 Scope:Host
     UP LOOPBACK RUNNING  MTU:16436  Metric:1
     RX packets:0 errors:0 dropped:0 overruns:0 frame:0
     TX packets:0 errors:0 dropped:0 overruns:0 carrier:0
     collisions:0 txqueuelen:0
     RX bytes:0 (0.0 B)  TX bytes:0 (0.0 B)
```

This system has two interfaces, eth0 and lo. The *lo* interface is the local loopback interface, present on every computer. It has no hardware, but is a logical interface the host uses to talk to itself. (Even Microsoft systems have this interface, although it doesn't appear in diagnostic output.) Some operating systems will show this as the loopback, or lo0, or something similar.

The more interesting interface is *eth0*, the network-facing interface. The first line tells us this is an Ethernet interface and gives its hardware (MAC) address. Below that we see the IP address, the top (unusable) address for the subnet this IP is on, and the netmask. Skipping the IPv6 entry, we see that this interface is UP (enabled) and has an MTU of 1500 bytes.

This particular version of `ifconfig` shows the number of packets sent and received, as well as send and receive errors. This is the same information as displayed by `netstat -i`. Yes, `ifconfig` displays some datalink information here, not just IP configurations. It breaks the clean separation of layers, in the interest of trying to tell you about problems. An interface accumulating errors has a physical or datalink layer problem, as discussed in Chapter 2. If you look at the interface errors on a wireless interface, you'll see why you shouldn't use wireless for servers.

On most Unix systems, the `route` command manages the system's routing table. The `-rn` flags tell the system to display the current routing table. Routes are usually displayed by address and netmask. The default gateway is identified by the word default or something like 0.0.0.0/0. Here's the routing table from a CentOS machine.

```
# netstat -nr
Kernel IP routing table
Destination Gateway      Genmask         Flags  MSS Window irtt Iface
0.0.0.0     203.0.113.1  0.0.0.0         UG       0 0         0 ens160
203.0.113.0 0.0.0.0      255.255.255.0   U        0 0         0 ens160
```

The first entry is our default route, pointing to the gateway at 203.0.113.1. The second entry is the route for the local network.

Solaris-based systems display the routing table with `netstat -rn -f inet` instead of the `route` command.

Multihoming and IP Aliases

Having multiple IP addresses on a host changes how the host interacts with the network. A host can have different interfaces on different subnets, attach multiple IP addresses to one network interface, or both. This is most common on servers, but you can do it on desktops as well.

A host can have two (or more) network interfaces, each with its own IP address, each in a different broadcast domain with different IP networks. Interface 1 might be on a public network and have an IP address of 192.0.2.2/28, while interface 2 might be on the private network and have an IP of 172.16.99.9/24. These interfaces could be virtual interfaces, as Chapter 2 discusses. Such a host is called *multihomed.*

A multihomed host automatically connects directly to hosts on subnets it's attached to, using its IP address on that subnet. Our example host connects to hosts on 192.0.2.0/28 using a source address of 192.0.2.2, and hosts on 172.16.99.0/24 with a source address of 172.16.99.9.

When leaving the local network, the multihomed host gives its outgoing traffic the primary IP address of the interface closest to the default gateway. If the host's default gateway is 192.0.2.1, traffic leaving the host for the Internet has the source address 192.0.2.2.

A host can have multiple IP addresses on one network interface through *IP aliasing.* The interface has a primary IP address, but it also answers ARP requests for the aliased IP addresses. Aliases are one way for a single host to communicate with multiple IP subnets on one physical Ethernet. The host initiates connections from whichever IP address it has on that subnet. Otherwise, all outgoing traffic comes from the primary IP address. Some programs allow the user to request a specific outgoing IP, but this requires explicit configuration or a command-line option.

Both IP aliasing and multihoming can be powerful tools. And both of them can cause huge problems. For example, enabling packet forwarding on a multihomed server transforms it into a router. Installing extra routers in your enterprise will make the network team demand your head on a stick as a warning to others. Before you deploy multihoming or IP aliasing in production, talk with experienced people about your use case.

Loopback and Localhost

All hosts have a *loopback interface*. This is a logical interface, with no hardware representation. It can only be accessed from the local machine, and can only be used to connect to the local machine. The loopback interface doesn't have an underlying layer 2, as it's a pure software interface. Every loopback interface gets the IPv4 address 127.0.0.1/8, the *localhost address*.

When a program wants to connect to something running on the local machine, it connects to the localhost address. Each computer can only connect to its own localhost interface and its own localhost address—that is, host A cannot connect to host B's loopback interface. Configuring a piece of software to connect to 127.0.0.1 is a sure way to make absolutely certain it connects to the local machine.

The whole 127.0.0.1/8 network is reserved for localhost connections. Yes, IPv4 addresses were much more plentiful way back when. Some operating systems attach additional addresses in that subnet to the loopback interface, for operational reasons.

Private Addresses and NAT

The purpose of an IP address is to let Internet hosts find each other. Not all hosts need to be accessible from the public Internet. Your average corporate desktop doesn't need to be reachable from the Internet—your security officer would probably have a fit at the idea. Your organization doesn't need an IP allocation from your ISP for those addresses.

You can't just grab random addresses for your private network. Your random addresses are probably in use elsewhere on the Internet, and if you use them on your private network you won't be able to communicate with that remote network.[9] Some addresses are reserved for special purposes, and trying to use them as regular network addresses breaks applications. If your organization runs an internal private network, they should use these dedicated addresses. Using public IPv4 addresses for a private network is an egregious waste of resources.

Various Internet bodies have set aside three subnets for use on private networks. You cannot use them on the public Internet, but anybody can use them on a private network. The networks 10.0.0.0/8, 172.16.0.0/12, and 192.168.0.0/16 are freely usable by organizations. You'll see these addresses in huge organizations and home networks, and have probably encountered some of them already. These addresses are also globally unique, *within your organization*. Your hosts should never see these addresses elsewhere, and other networks should never see these addresses on your network.

If a host only has private addresses, how do you access the Internet? Use either a proxy server or NAT. Both of these use multihomed hosts with one interface on the private network and a second that connects to the public Internet. (On complicated networks, these devices might have more than two interfaces.)

---

9   What are the odds you'll need to connect to those addresses? Eventually, one in one.

A *proxy server* accepts requests for Internet resources, hopefully sanity-checks the request, and requests the resource on behalf of the client. Take a web browser set to use a proxy server. When you try to get a web page, the browser contacts the proxy. The proxy asks the web browser to hold on for a moment, then requests that page on your browser's behalf. The proxy performs any filtering necessary and returns the sanitized page to the browser. A proxy server can be very secure, but it limits the Internet activity users can perform. Not all network protocols can go through a proxy.

Network address translation, or *NAT*, rewrites packets in flight. When a host with a private IP address sends traffic through a NAT device, the NAT device rewrites the outbound traffic so that it appears to be coming from the NAT device's public IP address. When the remote site answers, the NAT device rewrites the response so that it goes to the original client. The NAT device maintains a table of connections, and tracks the state of each connection so that it can properly open and close connections as needed. Most home routers are NAT devices. While NAT seems easy, it involves lying to all sides of a network connection, and not all protocols can handle those lies. Two common examples are FTP and VoIP, which both require special handling in NAT. The network administrator can apply filters to NAT devices to block some, but not all, unwanted traffic.

A *firewall* is most often some combination of packet filter, proxy server and NAT. Today, the word "firewall" means nothing in and of itself, although everyone uses the term. Every desktop comes with firewall software, which is a different critter entirely from the million-dollar devices protecting assorted Fortune 50 companies. Some firewalls are glorified NATs, others are proxies, and some offer both feature sets, with varying degrees of reliability and security.

While the word "firewall" might lack specific meaning, an organization absolutely has to have at least one. The type of firewall depends entirely on the organization. A one-man company might be able to function just fine with a desktop firewall. A big organization needs the heavier versions. Global organizations probably need many big firewalls. Part of the job of a company's security team is assessing what kind of firewall fits the company.

Proxies, NAT devices, and firewalls are not "Internet security systems." They are components in an organization's security policy, but the devices on their own are merely points of policy enforcement. NAT in particular is not a security mechanism—intruders broke the minimal protection NAT offers decades ago. You must have network border security, but an organization entirely reliant on its network border for security has already been broken into and doesn't know it yet.[10]

Troubleshooting IP

The two main tools for troubleshooting IP connectivity are `ping` and `traceroute`. Ping is mostly appropriate for connectivity tests on the local network, but it can also do extremely simple connectivity checks on remote networks. `Traceroute` is for troubleshooting connectivity to networks other than those on your local Ethernet broadcast domain. Chapter 12 is dedicated to `traceroute`. Chapter 2 discusses `ping`.

Now that you understand something about IPv4, IPv6 addressing won't seem so hard.

---

10   That's a strong statement for a sysadmin to make, but I stand by it. Read Richard Bejtlich's security books, notably *The Practice of Network Security Monitoring*, *The Tao of Network Security Monitoring*, and *Extrusion Detection*, to learn how to detect where your network has been penetrated.

Chapter 4: IPv6

The Internet started as a research and military network, back when computers cost millions of dollars and filled large specially-designed rooms. 4.29 billion addresses seemed like enough to last forever. The Internet's designers didn't expect people to do anything like give everyone in the industrialized world more than one networked computer, or connect banks to the Internet, or create a social media site where everyone would re-post the same fifty goofy cat videos over and over again. I mean, that's just ridiculous, right?

So we have 4.29 billion IPv4 addresses. Even without losses from subnetting, that's less than one address per human being. It's not enough.

Since the Internet was designed only for big institutions, the designers issued large blocks to large organizations. The Xerox Corporation has every IP address beginning with 13. HP has every IP address beginning with 15 and 16, Apple every IP beginning with 17, and the Ford Motor Company every address beginning with 19. (I know at least one of these organizations uses less than one percent of their space in public.) These are large organizations, but by modern standards they have far more addresses than they need.

The American Registry for Internet Numbers, or ARIN, projects that they will no longer be able to issue IPv4 addresses to new applicants on 23 April 2015. While it's possible that IPv4 address resale will extend the protocol's life, and NAT has extended IPv4's life far beyond any previous expectations, large parts of the world are already hurtling towards the replacement protocol, IP version 6.

Even if you don't need IPv6 today, one day your organization will discover a critical business need for it. Your network team is probably already pondering an IPv6 plan. I strongly recommend you prepare yourself now, rather than discover that you needed to deploy a completely unfamiliar protocol last month or last year. Today you have the luxury of learning slowly and in your own time. Next year, you might get it shoved down your throat with thirty minutes warning.

IPv6 Essentials

Like IPv4, IPv6 is a network layer protocol. IPv4 has 32-bit addresses, usually expressed as four groups of decimal numbers like 203.0.113.88. IPv6 uses 128-bit addresses, shown as eight colon-separated groups of four hexadecimal characters, such as 2a03:2880:2130:cf05:face:b00c:0:1 (the IPv6 address for a major social network's web site). With 128-bit addresses, every atom on Earth (including those in the lump of iron in the middle) can have 10 IP addresses. All the usual TCP/IP transport layer protocols can run atop it, as we'll see in Chapter 5. At the datalink layer IPv6 uses Neighbor Discovery (ND) rather than ARP, but as Chapter 2 shows, they have an awful lot in common.

IPv6 has a huge amount in common with IPv4. You can *almost* replace an IPv4 address with an IPv6 address and watch everything work. Applications use the IP address 2001:db8::1 just as readily as 192.0.2.1, provided the author wrote the software correctly. You'll find edge cases, of course, but for the average sysadmin IPv6 works almost exactly like IPv4.

One interesting difference between IPv4 and IPv6 is that in many operating systems, the last part of the host's IPv6 address can be computed from the network card's physical address (MAC address). Some people objected to this as a violation of privacy, so this behavior has gradually been replaced with non-reversible ways to generate IPv6 addresses, and there's discussion of obsoleting the reversible method.

In addition to the primary address, a host can have many temporary IPv6 addresses. The host can use these temporary addresses for outgoing connections. This partially addresses the privacy issues of tying an IP address to a piece of physical hardware. Instead of counting on protocols to provide privacy, it's best to remember that the Internet provides very little privacy without heroic measures. Handle sensitive and confidential information carefully!

Writing IPv6 Addresses

IPv6 addresses are long: 128 bits written as eight colon-delimited groups of four hexadecimal characters. As with IPv4 addresses, don't list the leading zeroes in each group. 2001:db8:000c:0000:0000:0000:00 0d:0001 looks even worse than 2001:db8:c:0:0:0:d:1.

The way that IPv6 manages and assigns subnets leads to addresses with long strings of zeroes. You can drop leading zeroes from any four-hex section. When an IPv6 address includes multiple blocks of zeroes, you can replace the longest string with two colons. The address 2001:0db8:000c:0000:0000:0000:000d:0001 usually appears as 2001:db8:c::d:1. Only do the double-colon replacement once per IP address, however, because otherwise it's ambiguous. Would 2600::c::d represent 2600:0:0:c:0:d or 2600:0:c:0:0:d? There's no way for the computer to tell, so don't do it.

IPv6 Netmasks

IPv6 is normally subnetted only at colon boundaries. Colons appear every 16 bits, so the natural IPv6 subnets are /16, /32, /48, and /64. The IPv6 standards recommend using /64 as the standard network on a small network like an office LAN or your home. A /64 contains 2^{64} IP addresses, more than enough for any Ethernet broadcast domain. IPv6 netmasks almost always appear in slash notation, but sometimes you'll see the words *prefix length* instead.

An average enterprise would receive a /48, divisible into 65,536 /64 subnets. If your company isn't a large telecommunications carrier but needs more than 65,536 subnets, someone needs to rethink their network design.

IPv6 Autoconfiguration

One interesting thing about IPv6 is that basic network configuration is built into the protocol. IPv6 clients on a /64 network automatically learn their IPv6 address, and the router's, through *router discovery*. Sadly, IPv6 autoconfiguration does not support assigning DNS servers or the options used for VoIP phones and other dumb devices, so they either need to be set manually or through IPv6 DHCP, or DHCPv6.

Servers that require static addresses should be careful with IPv6 autoconfiguration. An IPv6 host can support multiple addresses through IP aliases, just like an IPv4 host, and can be multihomed. If you use autoconfiguration to permit functions like changing routers without downtime, add an alias for the static IP address.

Localhost Address

Like IPv4, IPv6 has an address for "the local host." This address is ::1. Every host can connect to itself on this address.

IPv4 dedicates a whole /8 for localhost addresses. IPv6, more sensibly, uses only the single address.

Link-Local Addresses

IPv6 networks autoconfigure themselves, even without a router present! If a host capable of IPv6 connects to a network, it presents an IPv6 address to the network. All addresses beginning with `fe8` are *link-local addresses*, valid only on that specific interface's broadcast domain. IPv6 hosts on that Ethernet network can find each other and communicate via the link-local address. Link-local networks are always /64 networks.

Link-local IP addresses are not globally unique. The link-local network attached to the first Ethernet interface is a different link-local network than the one on the second Ethernet interface, and can include the same IP addresses. The operating system attaches the interface name to the link-local address so it can tell them apart. A link-local address usually appears with a percent sign and the interface name or number at the end of the address, such as we'll see in the next section.

If we have a nearly infinite supply of globally unique IPv6 addresses, what use are link-local addresses? Link-local addresses have many theoretical advantages, but for the practical-minded, they make standalone IPv6 networks self-configuring. You probably have IPv6 working in your home and don't know it. When I first set up IPv6, I was shocked to discover that my TV had always accessed my home NAS over link-local addresses rather than the static IPv4 addresses I'd assigned to them.

Viewing IPv6 Addresses

Like IPv4 addresses, use `ifconfig` and `ifconfig` or `ip` to view an interface's addresses.

ipconfig

Realistically, you'll want to use the `/all` flag to see IPv6 information. (I trimmed some irrelevant information from the output below.)

```
> ipconfig /all


Ethernet adapter Local Area Connection:

Description . . . . . . . . : Realtek PCIe GBE Family
Controller
DHCP Enabled. . . . . . . . : Yes
Autoconfiguration Enabled . : Yes
IPv6 Address. . . . . . . . :
   2001:db8::bd42:8975:8156:c112(Preferred)
Temporary IPv6 Address. . . :
   2001:db8::b8fc:3a1e:8c82:f265(Preferred)
Link-local IPv6 Address . . :
   fe80::bd42:8975:8156:c112%12(Preferred)
IPv4 Address. . . . . . . . : 203.0.113.72(Preferred)
Subnet Mask . . . . . . . . : 255.255.255.0
Default Gateway . . . . . . :
   fe80::d6ca:6dff:fe1a:dc68%12
```

This interface shows that Autoconfiguration Enabled is set to Yes. This interface will attempt IPv6 autoconfiguration. The "IPv6 Address" is the host's main IPv6 address, while the "Temporary IPv6 Address" can be used for outgoing connections to handle privacy concerns. The Link-local IPv6 Address ends in %12, showing that this address is local to interface number 12.[11] (Windows numbers interfaces automatically.)

Finally, the host's IPv6 default gateway appears above the IPv4 default gateway. It uses the link-local address of the gateway router rather than the autoconfigured one.

---

11   ipconfig shows only five interfaces. Some operating systems have spooky ghost interfaces.

ifconfig and route

Unix systems should show their IPv6 interface configuration right next to their IPv4 configuration. Again, here's some trimmed sample output from a Debian system.

```
# ifconfig
eth0      Link encap:Ethernet  HWaddr 00:0c:29:04:23:4c
   inet addr:203.0.113.206  Bcast:203.0.113.255  Mask:255.255.255.0
   inet6 addr: 2001:db8::20c:29ff:fe04:234c/64 Scope:Global
   inet6 addr: fe80::20c:29ff:fe04:234c/64 Scope:Link
```

This host has an IPv6 address of 2001:db8::20c:29ff:fe04:234c/64. You can tell it's a globally unique address by the trailing `Scope: Global` at the end of the address. The next line shows the link-local address.

Some operating systems, such as OpenBSD, don't enable IPv6 by default. They will not show any IPv6 information in `ifconfig`.

If your Linux system doesn't have `ifconfig` installed, use `ip address show` instead.

Many Unix systems display their default IPv6 route when you look at the IPv4 routes. If you want to view only the IPv6 routes, use `route -rn -A inet6` (Linux) or `route -rn -f inet6` (BSD).

Solaris-based systems display the routing table with `netstat -rn -f inet6` instead of the `route` command.

IPv6 Network Address Translation

Network Address Translation was created to work around the shortage of IPv4 addresses, letting a network administrator proxy lots of private addresses through a small number of public addresses. It's not part of IPv6, despite many organizations clamoring for its inclusion.

Why was NAT consciously and deliberately excluded from IPv6?

There's a common idea that NAT is a security measure. It's not. While NAT had minimal security advantages, those advantages vanished decades ago. IPv6 network hardware offers all of the advantages of NAT without lying to the network and breaking various applications. The idea that that NAT is a necessary component of network security is deeply entrenched, however.

IPv6 does have features that change IP addresses in flight, such as prefix translation. These are for redundancy or routing or resilience, however, not security.

Tunnels

IPv6 connectivity is most limited in areas where IPv4 is most widespread. North American and Western European organizations gobbled up most of the IPv4 addresses, so they experience less pressure from the IP address shortage than the rest of the world. This means that other parts of the world have implemented IPv6 more quickly than we have. As a result, the most remote parts of Africa and China might have better IPv6 connectivity than a large office building in London or New York.

Organizations like Hurricane Electric offer IPv6 *tunnels*, allowing a network or organization to get IPv6 connectivity over an IPv4 connection. These tunnels let you test IPv6 in your environment before your ISP offers it.

The biggest problem with tunnels is that they're bandwidth-constrained. Even if your organization has lots of Internet bandwidth, a tunneled IPv6 connection must traverse your IPv4 connection, go to the tunnel provider, and then out to the Internet. IPv6 tunnels are slower than native IPv6 connectivity.

Do you want to offer your company web site over an IPv6 tunnel? Perhaps. While the free tunnel providers are intended for experimenters and developers, you can get a commercial tunnel from a local provider. It will be slightly slower than a native IPv6 connection from your ISP, but depending on your use case that might be all right.

Be aware that your tunneled web site might get more traffic than you expect, thanks to the way IPv4 and IPv6 stacks interoperate.

IPv4 versus IPv6

Hosts can run with only IPv4 enabled, in which case they only talk to IPv4 hosts. They can use an IPv6-only configuration, which means they only communicate with IPv6 hosts. Things become more complicated when a host is *dual-stacked*, or configured to use both IPv4 and IPv6. What happens?

If a host uses both IPv4 and IPv6, incoming connection requests get processed via the protocol that they arrive on. An IPv4 connection request is answered in IPv4. IPv6 connection requests get IPv6 replies.

Outgoing connections can use either IPv6 or IPv4, depending on the operating system.

Microsoft Windows Vista and later prefer IPv6 if configured. Microsoft offers patches that control IPv6 and IPv4 preferences.

Unix systems vary widely in how they prefer one protocol over the other. Some, like OpenBSD and some Linux variants, rely upon DNS to decide if they're going to use IPv4 or IPv6. If the host's DNS client returns IPv6 addresses, the host uses IPv6. If the DNS returns IPv4 addresses, the host uses IPv4. Configure the address family search order in `/etc/resolv.conf`, by listing OS-specific keywords in the desired order.

Other operating systems, such as FreeBSD and other Linux versions, use a program like `ip6addrctl` or a file like `/etc/gai.conf` to set IPv4 and IPv6 preferences.

Which protocol is a better preference? That depends entirely on your IPv4 and IPv6 connectivity. You'll need to ask your network administrator how well each works on your network. If you have native IPv6, preferring IPv6 is fine. If you're getting IPv6 over a tunnel and you prefer IPv6, however, the host will send every network request over the tunnel. This makes everything run slowly and annoys users.

Not all hosts need the same protocol stack preference. If you want to have IPv4 as the default protocol in your production environment and IPv6 in a development area, that's fine. Do what works for your organization.

Now that you understand the network layer, let's go up to where the magic happens: transport!

Chapter 5: TCP/IP

The most popular Internet protocol is called TCP/IP. TCP (Transport Control Protocol) is a specific transport protocol that runs over IP, but the name TCP/IP refers to the whole family of protocols related to TCP and IP: ICMP, UDP, and TCP itself, as well as less common protocols like SCTP and ESP and AH and dozens of others.

Transport protocols run over both IPv4 and IPv6. They're slightly different on each IP version, with various headers updated to match the underlying stack, but the basics remain unchanged. That is, while TCP on IPv4 is not identical to TCP running on IPv6, concepts like port numbers and connection states remain unchanged.

A single chunk of TCP, UDP, or ICMP data is called a *segment*. Each segment gets wrapped in an IPv4 or IPv6 packet, which is then wrapped in a datalink frame and sent out into the cold hard world. The word segment isn't used very often. Instead you'll see references to a UDP or TCP packet, which means an individual segment wrapped in an IP packet. The IP packet contains vital information, like the source and destination IP addresses. Think of a segment like a fast-food hamburger in wax paper. If a cashier dropped a fresh hot burger, unwrapped, straight in your hand, you'd consider it incomplete.

I'll talk briefly about ICMP first, then proceed to UDP and TCP.

ICMP

The Internet Control Message Protocol (ICMP) transmits availability, routing, and status messages. While it's best known for tools like `ping` and certain `traceroute` implementations, ICMP includes all sorts of different messages. ICMP is almost as diverse as the more widely understood TCP and UDP protocols. While systems administrators don't need to know much about ICMP, you should know that it's there and it includes many different things.

ICMP is a vital part of the Internet infrastructure. Don't block it. Even blocking pings to obfuscate your network is of dubious utility, as intruders have so many other ways to investigate your network.

ICMP for IPv4 and IPv6 transmit similar types of messages, but internally they're completely different.

UDP

User Datagram Protocol, or *UDP*, is the most minimal transport protocol available in TCP/IP. The protocol considers each UDP packet self-contained, and while each packet has its own checksum, the protocol doesn't do anything to verify a flow of data as an entity. UDP is used for applications that do their own data flow error management.

A host that transmits a UDP packet has no way to tell the sending application if the packet ever reaches its destination. If the network drops a UDP packet, neither the sending nor receiving UDP layers in the operating system ever know. An application that's expecting a packet might notice and ask the sender to resend, but that's the application's responsibility.

UDP is called *connectionless* because a UDP data "stream" isn't really a stream: it's a whole bunch of independent packets that just happen to be traveling in the same direction. The packets have no defined order. Each is complete in and of itself. UDP packets are as connected as cars on a crowded freeway—they all travel at about the same speed and in the same direction, but they're independent. If one car blows its transmission and pulls over, nobody else cares.

Each UDP packet is wrapped in an IP packet that includes its source address, among other things. As each packet is considered a discrete entity, and has no relationship to other packets, this source address is easily forged. That's part of why your network team heavily filters UDP at the network borders.

So, UDP is easily faked, doesn't notice dropped packets, and doesn't check the data stream integrity. Why would anyone use this protocol?

UDP lets applications build their own error correction mechanisms tuned exactly to that application's needs. Some applications don't care about the occasional missed packet. If you're making a voice call over IP and the phone drops a couple of packets, you don't want the application to say "Oh, we lost a quarter-second of audio! I better go ask the sender to retransmit those!" No. The little slice of sound is gone. The caller doesn't need a two-second-old dropped slice of sound suddenly dumped into a blank spot in the conversation. That's how fights with your spouse start. Move on.

Almost all VPNs use UDP, although some use special VPN-specific protocols like IPSec. The protocols running over the VPN manage all necessary error correction, so the VPN doesn't need to handle those itself.

UDP is also really fast. You could be really fast too, if you didn't bother setting up connections or doing error correction.

If you need a protocol that handles all of the reliability stuff for you, you need TCP.

TCP

The Transport Control Protocol (TCP) includes much of the error correction that UDP lacks. The receiver acknowledges every single packet it receives. The sender retransmits any packet that isn't acknowledged. The packets have a very specific order, and the operating system verifies the integrity of the data stream. Applications that run over TCP expect the operating system to deliver exactly the traffic that was sent.

Treating a flow of TCP traffic as a whole makes TCP a *connected* protocol. Where UDP is like a crowded freeway, TCP is more like an automated factory. Every piece is tracked and assembled into a coherent whole. If a component falls off the assembly line, the robots slot in a replacement.

TCP is also a connection-oriented protocol, meaning that a chunk of application data can be broken into several TCP packets and streamed across the network as a single entity. The receiving operating system is expected to deliver the data in that stream of packets exactly as it was sent. Network routers and switches can send packets out of order—they shouldn't, but it happens. This means that a sender might transmit a data stream as several packets, but the packets might arrive at their destination in incorrect order or even broken up into smaller packets. The receiver gathers all the packets, puts them back in order, and assembles the stream into a coherent entity before handing it to the application.

Hosts exchanging TCP data must set up a connection for that data to flow across. One host requests a connection. The destination host either accepts, rejects, or ignores the request. If the destination accepts the request, it sends back information on how to connect. When the first host acknowledges the receipt of that information, it can start transmitting actual data. This setup process is called the *three-way handshake*. Similarly, once both hosts finish with the connection they must go through a little dance to tear it down, the *four-way handshake*.

TCP has fairly generic timeouts and transmission settings. If those values correspond to what an application protocol needs, it probably uses TCP. Applications that use TCP include web browsing and email. If you don't want TCP's settings, you need UDP or another protocol. VoIP, for example, can't work well with retransmissions and a two-minute timeout—human beings won't put up with that during a conversation.

Protocol Roles and Troubleshooting

ICMP, TCP, and UDP all have separate roles in the network, but they are highly interdependent. Combined with IP, ARP, and ND, they make everything work. No network performs well if any one of them fails.

Think of the network as a conference room. At the physical layer you have a table and chairs. The room is a broadcast domain. Each chair is a host, with a unique MAC address.

The table can hold a number of chairs equal to a power of two, as an IP network. Each chair has a unique IP address. The room's door is the default gateway. Two of the chairs, the top and bottom addresses, are rickety and dangerous to use.

ICMP lets you see things like "George's is asleep, so he's not answering questions." TCP is when you pass the stack of memos to the next person and make sure the other person has them before letting go. Drop the memos and you get to gather them off the floor and retransmit. UDP is when you crumple the memo into a wad and launch it at the project manager. What comes back might be the same memo, nothing, your termination notice, or a brick, depending on your meeting protocol.

The key to network troubleshooting on servers is to figure out which layer things broke at. Say Fred's not accepting the box of donuts and passing them on. If it's because he's busy fiddling with his phone and not accepting new connections, that's a local system problem. If his chair fell over backwards, that's a network problem. If Fred has already accepted more donuts than his stomach can handle, that's a local capacity issue.

Looking at the network isn't as easy as looking around a table. That's where the tools in the rest of this book come in.

Logical Ports

TCP and UDP both use *logical ports* to multiplex connections between machines, permitting one host to serve many different services to many hosts. When a network service like a web server starts it attaches, or *binds*, to one or more logical ports. A logical port is a number between 0 and 65,535, for a total of 65,536 ports.[12] TCP and UDP logical ports are separate things, although they use the same ranges of port numbers.

Each common Internet service has a standard port. Email services run on TCP ports 25 and 587. Web requests use TCP port 80, and SSL web requests use TCP port 443. UDP port 514 is used for log messages, while TCP port 514 is assigned to remote shell.

These port numbers are not physical constants or hard-coded into software, but rather mutually agreed upon. The only reason web servers run on port 80 is that everyone agrees that they do. DNS servers use port 53 for both TCP and UDP, but that's only because human beings have squishy organic data retrieval systems that randomly lose stuff. You certainly can run a web server on a different port, but you might have problems in certain organizations.

---

12   Chuck Norris can listen on port 65,536.

The Internet Assigned Numbers Authority, or IANA, maintains the authoritative list of port assignments. They're also responsible for many other Internet numbers, like IP addresses. Check their web site at www.iana.org for the most complete assignments.

Source and Destination Ports

Every connection comes from a port and goes to a port. If your desktop wants to connect to a service on a server, it picks a high-numbered port on the desktop and sends a packet to the service's port on the server. This is reversed on the other server—one machine's source port is the other's destination port. Every live connection has a unique combination of source and destination port.

Say you call up a web page. Your desktop might pick port 50,000 as a source port. It sends a request to port 80 on the web server. The server accepts the connection, and sends its response back to port 50,000 on the client, using port 80 as the source port. Port 80 on the server's IP address and port 50000 on the client's IP address now represent a single connection.

Another host could also use port 50,000 as its source port when it connects to port 80 on the same server, so long as it had a different IP address.

This unique combination of ports and IP addresses permits multiplexing of connections. A client that wants to make 10 separate connections to a web site can, so long as it uses ten different source ports. Combining source and destination IP addresses with separate source and destination ports creates a unique identifier for each connection.

The server tracks those connections using the same combination of IP addresses and ports. From the server's perspective, it's sending traffic from port 80 to lots of other ports and addresses.

Clients normally originate connections from high-numbered ports not assigned for other purposes. IANA recommends using port numbers 49,152 to 65,535 for these *ephemeral* ports. FreeBSD and newer versions of Windows use the recommended range, while most Linuxes use ports 32,768 to 61,000. Check your operating system documentation to change its ephemeral port range.

Combining Ports and IP Addresses

In IPv4, you commonly identify an IP address and port combination by printing the IP address, a colon, and the port. 192.0.2.66:80 means port 80 on the host 192.0.2.66.

IPv6 uses colons as a delimiter, so using a colon to separate the port from the address is easy to miss. The double-colon compression used in IPv6 addressing makes this worse. When you see 2001:db8::bd42:8975:8156:c112:80, you won't realize the trailing :80 is a port number unless you're deliberately checking to see if the author is trying to slip something past you. The standard way to show IPv6 address/port combinations is to put the address in square brackets, like [2001:db8::bd42:8975:8156:c112]:80. If you want to put an IPv6 address and port in your web browser, you must include the brackets.

Not everyone respects this standard, however. Sometimes you'll see an IPv6 address, a period, and then a port number, which while not obvious isn't completely horrible. Some applications do use a colon between IPv6 address and port, however. Don't make your application do this unless you want people to actively loathe you.

The Services File

The services file (`/etc/services` on Unix, `C:\\Windows\System32\drivers\etc\services` on Windows) lists services commonly used on the machine and the logical TCP or UDP port they normally use. Some programs use this file to see what port they should bind to or query on. Applications like `tcpdump` (Chapter 9) use the services file to look up what service runs on a particular port and transport protocol. This file doesn't need to contain every combination of port and protocol, but each it includes gets one line. Here are the entries for port 25.

```
Smtp 25/tcp mail #Simple Mail Transfer
Smtp 25/udp #Simple Mail Transfer
```

Each line has 5 fields. The first is the name assigned to this port— in this case, `smtp`. The second and third fields give the port number and transport protocol. Port 25, for both TCP and UDP, is allocated to this service. The fourth field is a list of alternate names for this service—in this case, `mail`. The second line in this example, UDP port 25, doesn't show an alternate name. Finally, after a hash mark, we have comments and notes about the entry.

I just said that email runs over TCP ports 25 and 587. Why does this list UDP port 25 as also reserved for email? Human beings are easily confused, and there are over 65,000 logical ports, so back in the day people thought they'd just assign both ports to one protocol. Like many great ideas from the early days of the Internet, this idea has been reconsidered as the number of protocols exploded.

The services list does not chain you down. You can run almost any software on almost any port, provided the software lets you. I've run the server access programs SSH and Remote Desktop Server on ports commonly assigned to other services, specifically to let me evade poorly managed firewalls. Feel free to break the standards yourself, once you understand why the standards exist and how your change might affect others.

Some organizations have rules on which ports they permit. I worked for one firm with a global private network that allowed only ports 80 and 443 open across the internal enterprise. Running a web server on a nonstandard port meant opening a change request for hundreds of sites worldwide. That change was often requested, but never approved. Check into those rules before changing port numbers.

Sockets

A *socket* is a communication endpoint for a process. It's a virtual construction for plugging communication into.

Sockets are used in places besides the network. Both Windows and Unix have *local sockets*, which are system entities on the filesystem or in memory that accept connections from other programs. Inter-process communication (IPC) is another common socket protocol, but it's contained entirely in memory.

In TCP/IP, a socket listens for a network connection. Your web server running port 80 opens a socket on port 80. One process can open any number of sockets, unless the operating system objects. The phrase *network socket* is another way to say "open TCP/IP port." A socket waiting for a connection is said to be an *open socket* or *listening*.

Unlike a physical socket, a network socket can accept any number of connections so long as all the clients have unique source IP addresses and ports.

Network Daemons and the Root User

Most Unix systems only permit the root account to open TCP and UDP ports below 1024. These *privileged ports* are normally assigned to the most popular or important Internet services such as web servers and email. Unprivileged users can run servers on higher port numbers. Services running on reserved ports are usually assumed to be vital and important. If a system accepts email, the system administrator better know about it! (This isn't great security, but it's a primordial Unix standard from the 1970s.)

If a piece of software is listening to the network, and an intruder compromises the software, the intruder gains access to the system as dictated by the user running the software. If your web server runs as an unprivileged user like www, an intruder can meddle with that user's files and processes. If root runs your web server, an intruder who breaks into your web site owns the whole system. You're in for a really bad day.

If you're running software that listens to the network as root: *stop it*. Investigate your platform's security features. Operating system developers offer all sorts of tricks to have software that listens to reserved ports run as unprivileged users. Some software starts as root but then drops privilege (*privilege separation*). Some operating systems give specific unprivileged users permission to listen to specific privileged ports.

An unprivileged user running the program attached to the socket should not have write access to that program's configuration file. You don't want, say, an intruder who breaks into your web server rewriting your web server configuration file.

Windows does not have reserved ports by default, but there's a registry setting to enable them. Network-facing Windows programs have no excuse for running as users like Administrator or System.

Reducing and restricting the privileges of users that can run network-facing servers is perhaps the biggest security improvement you can make on your servers.

TCP Connection State

Now that you know about ports, let's go into greater detail about TCP connection states. For a client and a server to communicate over TCP, they must set up a connection in a process called the three-way handshake. After they exchange data, they must tear down the connection. Each connection stage has a name.

The Three-Way Handshake

The first stage, a SYN request or SYN_SENT, is when a client requests a TCP connection from a server. (SYN stands for "synchronization request.") The request comes from a random high-numbered port on the client and goes to a specific port on the server.

At the second stage, SYN-ACK, the server responds to the SYN request. This is the server saying "I acknowledge your synchronization request, and include my own synchronization request." The response comes from the requested port on the server and goes to the client's source port. (If you have huge numbers of connections that never progress past the SYN-ACK stage, and you're getting more every second, you're under a SYN flood attack.)

The third stage, ACK, is when the client acknowledges the server's synchronization request. You need one SYN and one ACK in each direction. The connection is now ready to exchange data. The whole three-way handshake should take milliseconds, or possibly a second or two on slow, laggy, or overloaded links.

After the three-way handshake, the connection is ESTABLISHED. The client and server can exchange data as long as they can maintain a connection. The data for protocols like email, web, and instant message flow inside an ESTABLISHED TCP connection.

When the servers finish exchanging data, both sides request and acknowledge teardown. This is where you get states like CLOSE_

WAIT, TIME_WAIT, FIN_WAIT_2, and LAST_ACK. Expect to see these states linger until various OS-dependent timeouts expire.

TCP Failures

The network isn't perfect, and things occasionally go wrong. Network failures can break TCP. Problems can occur either on the server or on the network.

The TCP setup three-way handshake might fail. Perhaps the server doesn't listen on the requested port, or maybe a packet filter between the client and the server blocks the port or part of the handshake. A server or firewall might specifically reject or block the connection, creating a "connection refused" message on the client. The server or firewall might also silently ignore the request, and eventually the client will display a "connection timed out" message. If this happens, you can expect to see connections stuck in the SYN and SYN_SENT states.

If the client or server has a problem during the connection, they might send a *TCP reset* message. This means "I'm losing control of this connection, throw it away immediately." Higher level protocols get cut off. TCP doesn't do the teardown shuffle. While this can be caused by a firewall or a network issue, it's most commonly a server-side error. When an application is unceremoniously killed halfway through a transaction, its connections reset. Some network security devices send TCP resets to disrupt undesirable traffic.

More Protocols

TCP, UDP, ICMP, and friends are not the only network and transport protocols out there. The Internet supports or has supported hundreds of protocols. That's where the protocols file comes in. On Windows systems, look at *C:\Windows\System32\drivers\etc\ protocol*. On Unix systems it's */etc/protocols*.

Much like TCP and UDP logical ports, each protocol is assigned a number. Here's a small slice of the protocols file from one of my machines.

```
icmp 1 ICMP # internet control message protocol
...
tcp 6 TCP # transmission control protocol
...
chaos 16 CHAOS # Chaos
udp 17 UDP # user datagram protocol
```

Each line starts with the protocol name, in lower case. The second field is the protocol number. ICMP is protocol 1, TCP is protocol 6, and UDP is protocol 17. Any aliases for the protocol follow. Any comments are set off with a pound sign.

I've never seen most of the protocols in /etc/protocols, while some things in there surprised me. Protocol 16 is for "chaos?" The CHAOS protocol is old and no longer used, but it still has a protocol number assignment.[13]

The protocol number is used in TCP/IP headers, and appears when you analyze packets (Chapter 9) or write packet filtering rules (Chapter 11).

You now understand the basics of how the network is supposed to work. But how does this play out on real systems? Let's find out.

---

13   Chaos has ruled every organization I've been involved with. I never realized there was a protocol for it.

Chapter 6: Viewing Network Connections

Servers have IP addresses, and ports, and connections that might be over TCP or UDP or who knows what. How can you see which ports are open, which connections are live, and in general, what's going on?

That's where the `netstat` command comes in, along with tools like `lsof`.

The `netstat` program offers network statistics on both Windows and Unix systems. It lets you see which ports a server has open, current connections to other machines, and sometimes what's listening on a port.

Every operating system ships with `netstat`, but implementations vary. Some operating systems require add-on programs for basic functions. I give the Windows and Unix versions of `netstat` separate treatment when needed.

Hostnames and Netstat

By default, `netstat` attempts to use hostnames instead of IP addresses. This means your server performs a reverse DNS lookup on every IP address it exchanges traffic with. On a busy server, this might mean hundreds or thousands of lookups. Many hosts have no reverse DNS, so these lookups can take quite a long time before they fail.

Unix versions of `netstat`, along with Windows Server 2003 and newer, also use a human-friendly name instead of a port number whenever possible. It gathers this information from the services file. This results in a mix of named ports and numbers in `netstat` output, depending on whether a specific port has an entry in the services file.

All versions of netstat let you disable DNS lookups and port name lookups with the −n flag. I recommend almost always using −n. (I can't think of any exceptions, but I'm sure there is one. Somewhere.)

Netstat Display

Despite netstat running on different operating systems and all the various netstat implementers using slightly different command-line options and flags, netstat displays information in a surprisingly[14] consistent way.

Netstat Display Headers

You'll get netstat information in either four columns (Windows) or six (Unix). Here's the top of Windows' netstat output. All four of these columns also appear in Unix output.

```
Proto  Local Address        Foreign Address      State
TCP    0.0.0.0:135          0.0.0.0:0            LISTENING
TCP    127.0.0.1:49156      127.0.0.1:5354       ESTABLISHED
TCP    203.0.113.57:139     0.0.0.0:0            LISTENING
TCP    203.0.113.57:64692   203.0.113.201:445    SYN_SENT
...
```

The first column, *Proto*, shows if this entry involves TCP, UDP, or some other protocol. Different operating systems might display the IP version as well, such as TCP6 or UDP4, but that's clear from the context. This snippet shows four TCP connections.

The *Local Address* gives the IP address on the local system that this connection or socket uses, a colon, and the TCP or UDP port. For example, 127.0.0.1:80 means that this connection or socket is attached to port 80 on the IP address 127.0.0.1.

---

14   This is the first pleasant surprise I've had in writing this book. Or the previous book. Or, indeed, any tech book.

The *Foreign Address* column shows the IP address and port at the remote end of the connection.

Finally, the *State* shows what condition a TCP connection is in. Is this an active connection? Is it just closing down, or trying to start? Or is this a socket waiting for a connection? I discussed TCP connection states in Chapter 5.

Unix `netstat` inserts two columns in the middle, *Recv-Q* and *Send-Q*. These columns show the number of bytes the program's waiting to send to the socket, or the number of bytes received from the network that the kernel is waiting for the program to accept, or the number of bytes not yet acknowledged by the receiver. Low numbers in these columns are nothing to worry about, but if they start to climb then something has hung up.

Reading Netstat Entries

Each line of `netstat` output represents either one TCP/IP socket listening to the network or one live connection. Here are a few sample entries.

```
TCP   0.0.0.0:135   0.0.0.0:0   LISTENING
```

This entry uses the TCP protocol.

The local address 0.0.0.0 means "all IP addresses on this machine." If you add new IP addresses to this host, even without rebooting, this socket will be available on them. It's listening on TCP port 135, which the services file or an Internet search will show is the *epmap* protocol used for Microsoft-specific networking protocols. (BSD systems use a period rather than a colon to separate the port from the address.)

The foreign address is 0.0.0.0, which means "any address." Similarly, port 0 means "any port." How do you have a connection to any address and any port?

The fourth column holds the answer. The LISTENING state means that the software is waiting for an incoming connection. This is an open, idle socket.

BSD-based systems use * . * for the IP address of an idle socket on both TCP and UDP.

Here's a connection that's doing something.

```
TCP   203.0.113.57:51786   74.125.69.125:5222   ESTABLISHED
```

This is also a TCP connection. The local IP address is 203.0.113.57, and the local port is 51786. The remote IP address is 74.125.69.125, and the remote port is 5222. As this is a real connection, with real source and destination addresses, the operating system doesn't use the 0.0.0.0 placeholder. This connection is in the state ESTABLISHED, meaning that it's either passing data or ready to pass data.

```
TCP   203.0.113.57:6080   203.0.113.57:47245   TIME_WAIT
```

This TCP connection is from the IP address 203.0.113.57, but it's also to that same IP. This machine has connected to itself, which is not at all unusual. The state of TIME_WAIT means that this connection is finished and being torn down. Whatever happened here, it's done.

```
UDP   0.0.0.0:10001   *:*
```

Just when you thought you had this figured out, we switch from TCP to UDP. This looks different because the protocol is different. You should recognize the local address: this host is listening for incoming connections on all IP addresses, on port 10001. The remote address is *:*, which is UDP's way of saying "any IP, any port." Note the lack of a connection state. Remember, UDP is connectionless.

```
TCP   [::]:135   [::]:0   LISTENING
```

Wait—what happened to our IP addresses?

These are IPv6 addresses. The double colon means "any address," much like 0.0.0.0 in IPv4. Note the connection state of LISTENING. This is an open socket waiting for IPv6 traffic to TCP port 135.

Now that you know how to read the protocol, address, and port information, let's look at some specific examples from each operating system.

Windows Netstat

Windows `netstat` lets you view open ports, live connections, and what process is listening to a port.

Live Ports

Windows displays open ports and live connections with the `netstat -a` command. The output looks exactly like that under "Netstat Display Headers" earlier in this chapter.

On even a small laptop, this can generate hundreds of lines of output. I strongly recommend using a pager like `more`. (You'll need a modern terminal, not the MS-DOS Command Prompt.)

```
> netstat -na | more
```

A list of all open ports and active connections might be complete, but it contains far more than you're looking for. How do you narrow it down?

Show Only TCP or UDP

You can make Windows show only one transport protocol. Use the `-p tcp` modifier to make `netstat` show only TCP connections.

```
> netstat -na -p tcp
Active Connections

Proto  Local Address    Foreign Address     State
TCP    0.0.0.0:135      0.0.0.0:0           LISTENING
TCP    0.0.0.0:445      0.0.0.0:0           LISTENING
...
TCP    203.0.113.57:64692  203.0.113.201:445   ESTABLISHED
```

You might notice this only shows IPv4 TCP. Use -p `tcpv6` to show IPv6 TCP connections. Similarly, use -p `udp` and -p `udpv6` to view only those protocols.

Viewing Only Open Sockets

You might need to see only sockets, not live connections. View only listening sockets by combining `findstr` and `netstat`.

```
> netstat -na | findstr LISTEN
```

If you want to view only a particular protocol, add the appropriate -p arguments.

```
> netstat -na -p tcp | findstr LISTEN
```

The obvious question is: what service or program is creating these sockets?

What's Listening to the Network?

Identifying which programs or services are listening to the network requires elevated privileges. You can either start a command prompt as Administrator, or start an elevated PowerShell session.

Use the -b flag to print the name of the program or process using a connection or creating a socket.

```
> netstat -na -b
...
    TCP 0.0.0.0:135 0.0.0.0:0 LISTENING
    RpcSs
[System]
 TCP 0.0.0.0:445 0.0.0.0:0 LISTENING
    Can not obtain ownership information
    TCP 0.0.0.0:990 0.0.0.0:0 LISTENING
    WcesComm
...
```

Each port has one or two lines after it, listing the process holding the port open and, if it's there, the service responsible for that process.

Sadly, having one entry on multiple lines means that you cannot use findstr to grab only the entry you want. This is a case where grep is very useful.

Note the entry for the socket on TCP port 445. The netstat program can't figure out who owns the process. To see the process ID number, add the -o flag.

```
> netstat -na -bo
...
TCP 0.0.0.0:445 0.0.0.0:0 LISTENING 4
 Can not obtain ownership information
...
```

The new column, on the far right, shows the process ID number. That helps, somewhat, but how do you find out what process has PID 4? Run the tasklist command to display all tasks on the system, in order by process ID. It turns out that process ID 4 is always the System Service, the core of Windows, and is the usual cause of this message.

You can now see what your Windows box is presenting to the network. Let's turn to the Unix side.

Unix Netstat

Unix netstat programs vary by exact operating system. BSD-derived systems use one set of flags, Linux-based varieties another. Commercial UNIX usually follows one or the other. I cover BSD and Linux varieties of netstat here. Try both varieties on a commercial UNIX. If neither works, check your manual. The functionality is there, the vendor has merely changed the flags so that you renew your support contract.

Unix's netstat shows not only network connections, but also local sockets in memory and on the filesystem. This is valuable information, but it's not relevant to a discussion of networking. We'll add flags to remove this extraneous output.

89

Live Ports

To list every socket that's open on the system, whether it's a live connection or listening for an incoming connection, use netstat -a. Add -n to disable DNS lookups and port-to-name conversions.

On Linux-based hosts (and FreeBSD 11 and newer), use -4 to view IPv4 ports and -6 to show IPv6 ports.

On BSD-based hosts, use -f inet to view IPv4 ports and -f inet6 to view IPv6.

Here's a list of IPv4 connections and sockets on a CentOS host.

```
# netstat -na -4
Active Internet connections (servers and established)
Proto Recv-Q Send-Q Local Address     Foreign Address     State
tcp       0      0 127.0.0.1:25      0.0.0.0:*           LISTEN
tcp       0      0 0.0.0.0:22        0.0.0.0:*           LISTEN
tcp       0     64 203.0.113.205:22 203.0.113.57:50035 ESTABLISHED
...
```

The first line shows a TCP socket in the LISTEN state. This host is listening on IP address 127.0.0.1, port 25. This is a socket waiting for a new connection on port 25. As it's attached to the localhost IP 127.0.0.1, only programs on the local system can connect to it.

The second line shows a TCP socket, also in the LISTEN state. The local address is 0.0.0.0 port 22, meaning that it's listening to all available addresses on the host. This is a socket waiting for an incoming connection, either from the local machine or the entire Internet.

The last entry is also a TCP connection, but it has specific IP addresses and ports in both the local and foreign addresses. The ESTABLISHED state means this is a live, active connection. In this case, it's the SSH connection I'm actually running this command over. That's why there's data in the Send-Q column—I've run netstat, but my client hasn't finished acknowledging this data. There are 64 bytes in flight from the server to the client. By the time I see the entire netstat command, the client will have acknowledged this data. This queue will be back to 0. I can't see that zero, however. Every time I rerun this command, netstat and SSH queue a small amount of data.

If you don't use a command line flag to show only IPv4 or IPv6 sockets, you'll get all sorts of sockets: IPC, local, and network, plus anything else your system supports. Sorting through all that output is educational, but wait until you have a couple spare hours.

Show Only TCP or UDP

Linux-derived systems use −t to show only TCP connections and −u to show UDP. On BSD systems, use the −p argument and either tcp or udp. Here's the command to show open TCP ports and connections on an OpenBSD machine.

```
# netstat -na -p tcp
Active Internet connections (including servers)
Proto   Recv-Q Send-Q  Local Address      Foreign Address      (state)
tcp          0     64  203.0.113.204.22 203.0.113.57.50404 ESTABLISHED
tcp6         0      0  *.37               *.*                  LISTEN
tcp          0      0  *.37               *.*                  LISTEN
...
```

This shows both IPv4 and IPv6 connections. Add the IPv4-only or IPv6-only modifier to show only the TCP connections on a single protocol, as I do in this Debian example.

```
# netstat -na -t -4
Active Internet connections (servers and established)
Proto Recv-Q Send-Q Local Address Foreign Address State
tcp        0      0 0.0.0.0:47277 0.0.0.0:*          LISTEN
tcp        0      0 0.0.0.0:111   0.0.0.0:*          LISTEN
tcp        0      0 0.0.0.0:22    0.0.0.0:*          LISTEN
...
```

This list contains only IPv4 TCP sockets and connections.

Show Only Established Connections

Forget all of the listening daemons and such. What connections are established right now? The idea of "connections" only applies to TCP, so we can drop the -a flag from the netstat command. On BSD systems, use netstat -np tcp. For Linux, use netstat -t. Here I show a FreeBSD system.

```
# netstat -np tcp
Active Internet connections
Proto Recv-Q Send-Q Local Address     Foreign Address     (state)
tcp4      0     64 203.0.113.50.22 203.0.113.57.52661 ESTABLISHED
tcp4      0      0 203.0.113.50.22 203.0.113.57.50401 ESTABLISHED
```

This host has two established TCP connections. The local address is 203.0.113.50 port 22 for both. The remote address is 203.0.113.57 for both, but the remote port is different. I have two separate SSH connections into this machine. It's a good guess that the first one is the connection I'm using to run this command, because it queues up data to send when I run netstat.

Show Only Listening Sockets

Linux shows sockets that are waiting for a connection with netstat's -l flag. Here I list all IPv4 sockets listening for an incoming connection.

```
# netstat -ln4
Active Internet connections (only servers)
Proto Recv-Q Send-Q Local Address Foreign Address State
tcp       0      0 127.0.0.1:25  0.0.0.0:*        LISTEN
tcp       0      0 0.0.0.0:111   0.0.0.0:*        LISTEN
tcp       0      0 0.0.0.0:22    0.0.0.0:*        LISTEN
udp       0      0 0.0.0.0:1004  0.0.0.0:*
udp       0      0 0.0.0.0:111   0.0.0.0:*
```

This host is listening for incoming connections on TCP ports 22, 25, and 111, and UDP ports 111 and 1004.

BSD systems don't have the -1 option. You can do something approximately the same by excluding established connections.

```
# netstat -na -f inet | grep -v ESTABLISHED
```

The next question is: what daemon answers when a client attaches to that port?

What's Listening On That Port?

Unix does not have a cross-platform command to display what programs are listening to a port. All Unix variants give you a way to figure this out, but they're all different.

On Linux `netstat`, the $-p$ flag toggles showing the process ID and program name holding a port open. You probably want to combine this with other flags such as -4 (for IPv4), $-t$ (TCP), or $-u$ (UDP). Narrow it differently with -1 (shows only listening ports) or $-a$ (shows all ports). Here, I see what's listening to each TCP port on a Debian machine.

```
# netstat -ptln
Active Internet connections (only servers)
Proto Recv-Q Send-Q Local Address Foreign Address State   PID/Program
name
tcp      0      0 0.0.0.0:22    0.0.0.0:*       LISTEN 2360/sshd
tcp      0      0 127.0.0.1:25  0.0.0.0:*       LISTEN 2392/exim4
tcp6     0      0 :::22         :::*            LISTEN 2360/sshd
tcp6     0      0 ::1:25        :::*            LISTEN 2392/exim4
```

This host has an SSH daemon listening to the outside world on port 22, and exim4 listening on 127.0.0.1 and ::1 on port 25.

FreeBSD has a small program for viewing what program's holding sockets open, `sockstat`. Use -4 to view only IPv4 sockets and -6 to view IPv6. The output is very similar to `netstat`, but starts with the user and command using the socket.

```
# sockstat -4
USER       COMMAND PID     FD PROTO  LOCAL ADDRESS      FOREIGN ADDRESS
mwlucas    sshd    34561   3  tcp4   203.0.113.26:22    192.0.2.77:52217
spamd      perl    33362   5  tcp4   127.0.0.1:783      *:*
bind       named     894   8  tcp4   127.0.0.1:53       *:*
...
```

The user mwlucas has an established SSH connection from the Internet. (The local port is 22, which is the SSH port. This connection is coming from the IP 192.0.2.77 and a high-numbered port.) On localhost, the program `perl` is listening for connections on TCP port 783 and `named` is listening to TCP port 53.

If your Unix's `netstat` program doesn't offer an easy way to view which program is listening on a port, try `lsof`. Lsof is a general-purpose program for listing open files, but Unix treats network ports much like files. Not all Unixes include `lsof` out of the box, but every one of them has an `lsof` package. Use `lsof -i` to see all network ports in use, both listening sockets and established connections. Turn off DNS resolution with `-n`.

```
# lsof -n -i
COMMAND PID USER ... TYPE ... NODE NAME
syslogd 621 root ... IPv6 ... UDP *:514
sshd    754 root ... IPv4 ... TCP *:22 (LISTEN)
httpd   759 root ... IPv6 ... TCP *:80 (LISTEN)
...
```

I have removed some columns from the output, to make it fit on the page.

The first column shows the program name. The second column gives the process ID of the command, and the third gives the username running the command. For example, the first line shows that the user `root` is running `syslogd` as PID 621.

The TYPE column shows if this program is listening on IPv4 or IPv6. I have a mix of protocols here.

94

The NODE column shows if this is a TCP or UDP port.

Finally, the NAME column shows the port number.

`Lsof` is an incredibly useful program, and can provide you with huge amounts of visibility into your system. If you've never used it, I strongly encourage you to check it out.

You can now see which ports are open, which are in use, and the state of various connections. Let's move from passively investigating a machine's relationship with the network to actively poking at the network and seeing what pokes back.

Chapter 7: Network Testing Basics

As a systems administrator, you have an awful lot of access to the network. You have more access to network information than you think you do. You only need a few freely-available tools to test and view that information, and the knowledge to use them.

The goal of a sysadmin testing the network is to pinpoint a problem's source. Is an issue on the server, or on the network? Potential network issues for systems administrators boil down to two key questions: what do my hosts send, and what do my hosts receive?

A host needs to put data on the network. With the proper tools you can view exactly what data a host puts on the network and where it sends that data. You can also feed arbitrary data to the network.

Hosts also need to receive data. The expectation is that each host receives the data sent by its clients. If a client sends data, but it never arrives at the server, the problem lies between the two. If you see connections and/or data arrive at your server, but your server doesn't answer, examine your server. If the data sent by a client never arrives at the server, pick up the phone and call the network team.

The rest of this book focuses on two questions: what does a host transmit, and what does it receive? You can view and generate arbitrary traffic in both directions.

Network Testing Etiquette

The network exists to support the users and hosts. That doesn't mean sysadmins own the network. Be polite. If in doubt involve your network team before doing anything that might be intrusive.

As a general rule, you can always send normal traffic between machines you own. If you run the mail server, of *course* you can send test mails and configure clients. If you want to test connectivity between TCP ports normally used for email, that's *certainly* within your purview. Normal traffic, or traffic that resembles normal traffic, is always acceptable.

Abnormal network traffic is another story. The tools described here let you create small amounts of abnormal traffic. With a little investigation you can find tools that let you create very large amounts of very abnormal traffic. Abnormal traffic sets off the network team's alarms, or might even engage the network's intrusion detection and/or defense systems. Either of these events end with an aggrieved network engineer or manager at your desk, asking you what, exactly, you think you're doing. The two most common offenders are load testing and port scanners.

If you want to see how much bandwidth you can get between two servers, you're talking about network load testing. Good hardware running the right software can saturate a local network and cause problems for other hosts. A saturated network will set off the network team's alarms.

Once you get into network testing, you'll probably discover tools like port scanners. A port scanner is a wonderfully powerful tool. That's why intruders use them so frequently. They also tend to generate abnormal traffic. Firewalls and intrusion detection systems usually trigger when someone uses a port scanner on the network.

In some environments, generating abnormal traffic might get your server kicked off your own network. If it doesn't, it should at least set off alarms.

Setting off alarms makes other people not like you. Talk to your network team before generating abnormal traffic. They might want to run some of these tests for you, or have you run them at a scheduled time. These discussions always go better if you repeatedly demonstrate that you understand basic networking tools before trying something complex or intrusive like load testing or port scanning.

Reporting Problems

Assume that you have two hosts on separate parts of an enterprise network. They might be on different IP subnets, different broadcast domains in the same datacenter, or on different continents or hemispheres. Each host has connectivity to the rest of the enterprise, but not to each other. Traffic you send from one doesn't reach the other. What's going on?

Long-standing sysadmin tradition says "blame the firewall." This tradition causes all sorts of problems. Yes, you probably have a firewall on the network, and it might need a change to permit the traffic. But you might have a packet filtering router. Or a proxy server. Or maybe a load balancer. Or all of them. From a purely technical perspective, you might not really care what's blocking the traffic. Something's blocking your application, and you want the pain to stop.

On a human level, though, the difference is *vital*. Most people take things personally. When someone says "it's a server problem," many sysadmins hear "This is the system administrator's problem" or, worse, "the sysadmin is unworthy to receive today's oxygen ration."[15] It's illogical. It's human.

---

15   If you don't take anything personally, congratulations! I'm talking about other people. And you dress weird.

Network administrators feel the same. By blaming "the firewall," you're attaching blame to someone who might or might not have any bearing on the problem but who can make your life difficult in the future.

When packets change in transit or flat-out don't arrive, don't leap straight to blaming the firewall. Open a ticket with the network team that describes what you're sending and what you're not receiving. There's a great big world of difference between "connection refused" and "connection timed out," and giving the exact language of the error message can vastly accelerate problem resolution. Maybe it *is* the firewall team's problem, but maybe this time it's the router crew. And always include the time the problem happened, so that your system's errors can be correlated with other network events.

As the reverse side of this, let the other team know what you're trying to accomplish. You know how your own users will sometimes ask for solution A, but it eventually turns out that they're trying to accomplish task B, which you've already solved with tool C if they had known to ask for it? Don't do that to your other IT teams. Tell them what you're trying to accomplish. They might already have a tool or process for it.

Providing accurate information, and carefully avoiding anything that might be taken personally, accelerates troubleshooting more than any other technique I know of. Some people will always behave poorly, but this lets you separate the well-meaning but stressed and busy people from the actual jerks.

Exactly as in system administration, providing facts rather than leaping straight to diagnoses or conclusions accelerates solving the problem, which is all anybody cares about.

Network Manglers and Blockers

So what can block or disrupt traffic between two hosts? Here are the most common candidates.

A firewall is a common network access control device. Calling a firewall a security device is something of a misnomer. It's a point of policy enforcement, dictating what traffic may pass from one segment to another. Normally this control is based on TCP/IP ports and IP addresses and protocols. Servers can also have firewalls, usually software-driven. Be sure your own firewall isn't blocking traffic before calling the network team!

Common firewalls use a *default deny* policy. Everything is forbidden unless explicitly permitted. I've been on more than one enterprise network where the internal firewalls permitted ports 80 and 443 across the entire enterprise, but blocked all other traffic between global locations. Opening other ports between sites required firewall changes.

Firewalls are not the only devices that can control access to specific addresses, protocols, and ports. Most routers and many Ethernet switches can perform *packet filtering* or use *access control lists* (ACLs) to limit connectivity. From the sysadmin's perspective, a packet filtering router is exactly the same as a firewall. In a large enterprise, however, a different person or team manages it.

Sometimes traffic passes between the client and the server, but the content changes en route. You send a web request from a client, and although it arrives at the server the contents are mangled. Perhaps HTTP headers are added, moved, or changed, or maybe parts of the data are just missing. Something between the hosts is altering the data, probably a proxy server.

A proxy server inspects and sanitizes certain applications as they cross the network. While web browsers can be configured to use a proxy, some networks transparently intercept application traffic and route it to a proxy. Your application's traffic tripped something in the proxy. You'll need to talk to the people who manage that proxy to continue troubleshooting, but being able to say "Something between these two IP addresses is removing the fubar headers from my HTTP application" will shorten and simplify that discussion.

Last, you might contend with load balancers. A load balancer distributes network traffic between multiple hosts to share the burden between them. If you run a very popular web site, one web server can't handle that amount of traffic. A load balancer lets you use multiple web servers to support one site. Load balancers redirect TCP/IP connections as load dictates, and might also mangle the content to more intelligently redirect load. If you administer servers behind a load balancer, make friends with the load balancer administrator.

Now let's test your network without alienating anyone, starting with DNS.

Chapter 8: the Domain Name System

The Domain Name System (DNS) is a core feature that holds networks and the whole Internet together. Many people have never heard of it and many others have no idea how it works. A sysadmin doesn't need to understand the innards of DNS, but he needs to know the basic ideas behind it and how to query the system for information.

DNS provides a map between human-friendly hostnames (like www.mwl.io) and IP addresses like 192.0.2.8. Without DNS, you'd browse the web with IP addresses instead of hostnames. To most end users, a DNS failure means that the Internet is down. DNS is traditionally part of the network team's responsibility, often on Unix systems, although in some enterprises it's shared with or moved entirely over to the Windows administration team.

DNS is a complicated topic that fills books much larger than this one. I'm not giving you a detailed dive into DNS. Enough DNS knowledge to catch obvious common errors, or say "hey, this looks really *weird*" will help you a lot, however.

Perhaps you can't make changes to your organization's DNS information, but once you understand how the DNS works you can query it, find mistakes, and get them fixed.

DNS runs on TCP and UDP, using port 53 on both. It's a common myth that DNS only uses UDP, but that hasn't been true since the 1990s.

DNS Principles

DNS maps IP addresses to host names, and hostnames to IP addresses. Users don't care what a host's IP address is, they just want to type google.com into their browser and go. While you can hard-code host and IP information into a computer (see "The Hosts File," later this chapter), that isn't scalable or maintainable. Every network needs a DNS server, also called a *nameserver*, to gather this information for you.

A nameserver is a piece of software that searches for and collects address and hostname mappings. Whenever you visit a web page, your computer makes a DNS request to a nameserver. The nameserver checks its local cache to see if it already has an answer. If the nameserver has a cached answer, it sends the information to the client. If the nameserver doesn't have that information, it queries the Internet to get an answer and returns that answer to the client.

When configuring a computer, give it the IP addresses of your nameservers. If the host uses DHCP, it gets those addresses automatically. If you must set an IP address manually, you'll need to set DNS servers as well. You must always specify DNS servers by IP address, not hostname. A host can't look up hostnames until it can use DNS.

Some sites maintain their DNS entries by hand. Others use automatic configuration. Knowing which your organization uses will help you separate human problems from software errors.

Domains and Zones

You've seen domain names, like michaelwlucas.com and google.com. These are a specific type of DNS *zone*.

DNS is very hierarchical. Each level within the hierarchy is a zone. Every top level domain like .com and .net is a zone. Both michaelwlucas.com and google.com are zones. If I created a subdomain, like home.michaelwlucas.com, where I could put hosts like tv.home.michaelwlucas.com, the subdomain would also be a zone. All of the top level domains—.com, .net, and so on—are contained in the all-encompassing *root zone*.

A zone inside another zone is called a *child zone*. The zones michaelwlucas.com and google.com are both child zones of the .com zone.

A zone that holds other zones is a *parent zone*. The .com zone is a parent of many zones, including mine and Google's.

Which zone is a child and which a parent? That depends entirely on where you're standing. Just like people, one zone's parent is another zone's child. The .com zone is the parent zone of michaelwlucas.com, but .com is also a child zone of the root zone.

A complete collection of data for a zone is called a *zone file*. Zone files live on the authoritative DNS servers.

Authoritative and Recursive DNS

DNS servers come in two varieties: authoritative and recursive.

Authoritative nameservers contain the information for specific domains. For example, I run authoritative DNS for domains that I host, such as michaelwlucas.com. Anyone in the world who wants to perform DNS queries on my domains gets an authoritative answer from my servers.

Recursive nameservers provide DNS lookups for clients. When you browse to cnn.com, your computer asks a recursive nameserver for the IP address to connect to. (Strictly speaking, it's asking for the A record that contains the IP address, but we haven't talked about A records yet, so just go with it.) The recursive nameserver finds the authoritative nameserver for the destination site, queries it, and returns the answer to your computer. When configuring a server for network access, use the IP address of your local recursive server. Get this address from your network administrator.

Best practice says that authoritative and recursive nameservers should be on different machines. The long-running practice of combining authoritative and recursive DNS on one machine led to many security problems. While separate machines for these services was expensive in time and resources a few years ago, with virtualization it's really not a problem.

Some vendors insist on combining authoritative and recursive DNS in one installation. While dealing with all the hacking attempts that configuration gets is a great learning experience, I still encourage you to slap your account rep soundly until they stop.

The DNS Hierarchy

DNS is the world's most successful distributed database. Here's how it's distributed.

Suppose a client asks its nameserver for the IP address of a host. This information is not in the nameserver's cache.

The nameserver consults its list of root name servers, picks one, and asks it for information. The root nameserver says "I don't know about that host, but here are the authoritative nameservers for my child zone that the host is in. Go ask them." The nameserver requests those authoritative nameservers for information, and probably gets directed to another layer of authoritative servers. Each layer of subdomains means another layer of authoritative nameservers.

Eventually the recursive nameserver reaches a nameserver that says "I am the final authority on this host, and here is my answer." The recursive nameserver caches that answer and sends it back to the client.

How does this work in practice? Suppose you point your web browser at my web page, http://www.michaelwlucas.com. Your computer needs to know the IP address for that site, so it asks its nameserver for it.

Your nameserver has never heard of my site[16], so it asks a root server. The root nameservers know the DNS servers for every top level domain, like .com, .net, .biz, and so on. The root server says "I don't know, but here are the authoritative servers for .com." Your nameserver knocks at the authoritative servers for .com and says "Hey, do you know the IP for www.michaelwlucas.com?" The .com nameserver replies "I don't know, but here are the authoritative servers for michaelwlucas.com." Your nameserver queries the nameservers for michaelwlucas.com, and gets told "Here is the IP for that host."

If you have many subdomains, the chain of queries is much longer.

Forward and Reverse DNS

Forward DNS maps hostnames to IP addresses. The client requests the IP for mwlucas.org and gets an answer like 203.0.113.99.

Reverse DNS maps IP addresses to hostnames. The client requests the hostname assigned to the IP address at 203.0.113.99 and gets an answer like www.ignoredsince1993.net. (That is the real answer for that address, by the way.)

A forward DNS query can return more than one answer. As I write this, a DNS query for google.com gives me 11 IP addresses. A reverse DNS query should only return one hostname, however. (The standard allows returning multiple PTR records for a single IP address, but doing so breaks various security and reputation checks. If your network does this, that's almost certainly why your app failed—especially if it sends email.)

---

16   I am an incredibly well-kept secret, known only to the computing elite. Congratulations!

These maps don't have to correspond to one another. One IP address might support many domain names. Each of an ISP's web servers probably has hundreds or thousands of sites on it. A DNS query for any of those sites would lead to the host's IP address, but a reverse DNS query on that IP address would probably return a hostname like www87.example.com.

DNS Record Types

DNS' greatest curse is its success. DNS was designed as a general purpose configuration database, most widely used to map IP addresses to host names and back. It worked, so over the years people have jammed all sorts of interesting things into zone records. They got away with it, so people added more data types, and more, and more. DNS records can now tell a network phone how to find the local VoIP server and a desktop where to get LDAP services.

All of these different types of data go into different DNS record types. We're focusing on only the most common record types. Not all tools always show the record type, but if you see the record type you should know what it means.

An *A* (address) record contains an IPv4 address. If you have a hostname and want to find its IP address, your query should return an A record.

Similarly, an *AAAA* record contains an IPv6 address. If your client wants a host's IPv6 record, it will ask the nameserver for its AAAA record.

A *PTR* (pointer) record contains a hostname. When you have an IP address and want to know the hostname tied to it, the client requests a PTR record. Reverse DNS mostly uses PTR records, but PTR records also show up in other protocols like ZeroConf and Service Discovery.

An *SOA* (Start of Authority) record gives timing and responsibility information for the zone you're searching. It includes things like "how long should a recursive nameserver cache entries" and "who do I contact for problems with this domain?"

A CNAME (canonical name) is a DNS alias, redirecting one name to another.

An MX (mail exchanger) record identifies one of the mail servers for a zone.

You'll see other types of records, depending on the applications you support and your environment, but once you see where these appear and how they're used you'll be able to look them up on your own.

DNS Caching

Recursive DNS servers cache collected answers until a per-DNS-record timer expires. Once the answer expires, the recursive DNS server throws the data away. When a client wants the data again, the recursive server gets a new answer from the authoritative server. Even if a site's DNS administrator makes a change to her authoritative DNS, recursive nameservers will use the cached answers until they expire.

This means that DNS changes take time to propagate across the Internet. If your DNS administrator changes something, you must wait for the various caches to expire before clients get the new information. The propagation time depends on the domain's DNS configuration. Ask your DNS administrator how long propagation should take.

No matter what your DNS administrator does, though, some nameserver operators deliberately and consciously choose to ignore the DNS configuration and retain DNS data long after its expiration time. Your DNS administrator can't help people who deliberately break their servers this way.

Some operating systems run local DNS response caches. Windows, for example, automatically remembers recent DNS requests. Various Unixes might use a name service caching daemon like `nscd` for local name caching. You can flush local caches by restarting the Unix name caching daemon or running `ifconfig /flushdns` on Windows.

When you find incorrect DNS information, see if it's coming from the host's local cache, the recursive nameserver's cache, or the authoritative server.

When you suspect a DNS problem, check to see if you're getting an answer from a nameserver or a local cache.

All of this caching means that you must be very careful when changing a host's IP address. If you must change the IP address on a critical service, talk with the DNS administrator as far ahead of time as possible. The DNS administrator can change how long most clients will cache data for your servers, but she must make that change well in advance. She might need an hour's notice. She might need a month or more. It depends entirely on your environment. The only way to find out is to ask in advance.

Why Check DNS?

If the main points of network troubleshooting for sysadmins are verifying that you're sending and receiving traffic, why do you need to care about DNS?

A misconfigured DNS can send clients to the wrong host. If you have configured a web site on the host 198.51.100.99, but DNS claims that the web site is on the host at 198.51.100.222, clients will never reach your server. The DNS needs correcting.

The information you expect in DNS might be totally absent. In this case, when you try to send traffic, the client will fail before it transmits a single packet to the desired server. Your client won't send traffic to an unknown address. It will just shrug and give up instead.

While DNS can go wrong in many other ways, incorrect and missing information are the most popular problems.

Running DNS Queries

Windows provides the `nslookup` command for DNS debugging. On Unix systems, use `host`. Unix systems might include `nslookup`, but it's frequently an obsolete or deprecated version.[17] We'll consider each separately.

Both tool sets show the standard DNS response and error codes.

DNS Response Codes

DNS queries most often return three response codes: NOERROR, NXDOMAIN, and SERVFAIL. (There are more, but they're rare.) You'll get these from both Windows `nslookup` and Unix `host` commands.

NOERROR means that everything worked correctly. You ran a query and got a valid response. While the query ran without error, NOERROR does not mean that the information is correct—it only means that the DNS process worked and you got something back. The DNS might not give a useful answer—"I know nothing" is a valid answer. It might list the wrong IP for a host, but the DNS protocol itself worked. Some tools don't print NOERROR, but print only the answer provided. Others print NODATA when no valid answer is found.

NXDOMAIN means that the DNS protocol worked, but that the DNS doesn't contain any records of the name you're looking for. If you

---

17   Unix nslookup was the standard DNS query tool. Then it was deprecated, abandoned to rot, and then resurrected. Versions of nslookup in all of these states have been shipped with production operating systems. Don't trust any of them.

query DNS for the host wwww.cnn.com (note the 4 *W* characters, not three), you'll get an NXDOMAIN error. Your DNS got an authoritative answer; there is no such host.

SERVFAIL means that something went wrong, and you can't get an answer. Maybe the authoritative servers have lost their minds and stopped answering queries. Maybe DNS Security Extensions (DNSSEC) blew up. Maybe your local recursive server has gotten ill. Perhaps an incorrect record somewhere has made the whole system roll belly-up. You don't get an answer. You're not going to get an answer until something changes.

When you get a SERVFAIL or NXDOMAIN response, the first thing to check is your query. Did you type the IP address or host name correctly? When I run DNS servers, typos are the most common cause of problem reports—not just from systems administrators, but from everyone. Those extra Ws just keep creeping in!

Windows and nslookup

Windows ships with `nslookup`, a basic DNS query tool. `Nslookup` is generally regarded as obsolete, but Microsoft has kept their version more updated than most. Windows `nslookup`, unlike that in Unix systems, is perfectly adequate for basic DNS queries.

Let's start with a simple DNS query. Give `nslookup` a hostname and it will find its IP address. Here I look up the IP of my site.

```
> nslookup michaelwlucas.com
Non-authoritative answer:
Server:   google-public-dns-a.google.com
Address:  8.8.8.8

Name:     michaelwlucas.com
Address:  108.61.84.15
```

112

This is the simplest sort of DNS response you'll get. You ask a basic question and get a basic answer. My web site has only one server, and there's no content delivery network or redirection or anything complicated between us.

The response begins by telling us that this is a non-authoritative answer. That's normal whenever you're not talking directly to the authoritative nameserver. An answer from a recursive server is always non-authoritative.

Then we see which recursive nameserver it's talking to, by hostname and IP address. Here I'm using Google's public DNS servers, at 8.8.8.8.

`nslookup` reminds us what we asked for: my personal domain.

Finally we get what we asked for, the IP address of my web site. If I check my own DNS, the first thing I do is compare this address to the address I've assigned to my web server. If they match, DNS is correct. If they don't match, I go have words with my DNS administrator.

Let's look at a slightly more complex example, CNN's site.

```
> nslookup www.cnn.com
Server:   google-public-dns-a.google.com
Address:  8.8.8.8

Non-authoritative answer:
Name:     cnn-cop.gslb.vgtf.net
Addresses:  157.166.238.17
    157.166.239.177
    157.166.238.48
Aliases:  www.cnn.com
    www.cnn.com.vgtf.net
```

This bears a lot of similarity to the first query: we see the server we're querying and get IP addresses back. But CNN uses aliases in their DNS. Nslookup sees that www.cnn.com is an alias for the hostname cnn-cop.gslb.vgtf.net. It then spits out the addresses behind that alias. At the end, `nslookup` explicitly gives the aliases.

Reverse DNS queries should never get that complex. You don't get aliases and redirections in most reverse DNS. Run `nslookup` and use the IP address you want to look up as an argument.

```
> nslookup 108.61.84.15
Server:   google-public-dns-a.google.com
Address:   8.8.8.8

Name:     www.michaelwlucas.com
Address:   108.61.84.15
```

The bottom of the output shows the hostname assigned to that IP address.

You can do more complicated queries with `nslookup`. Perhaps you want to query a specific DNS server, rather than the first one configured on your system? Give the server name or IP address as a second argument. Here I query Google's second public nameserver (8.8.4.4) to see what it knows about my web site.

```
> nslookup.exe mail.michaelwlucas.com 8.8.4.4
```

It should return the same information as the primary nameserver.

You can also use `nslookup` interactively, so you can run several queries in a row with the same settings. Enter a plain `nslookup` at the command prompt to enter interactive mode.

The versions of `nslookup` shipped with Windows 8 and Server 2012 have been updated to support the newest protocol standards. You can extract useful, detailed information from the DNS with those versions. If you need to perform sophisticated DNS debugging, I would suggest you grab a copy of BIND or ldns for Windows and use `host` and either `dig` or `drill`.

Unix and host

The `host` program is the standard Unix DNS diagnostic program. Your Unix probably gets its version of `host` either from BIND or ldns. BIND is the long-running standard, while ldns is the newer competitor. While they're highly different internally, you can use either for basic troubleshooting.

Again we'll start with a simple example, my web site.

```
# host www.michaelwlucas.com
www.michaelwlucas.com has address 108.61.84.15
```

Your simple question got a simple answer. If you want more detail in your answer, add -v.

```
# host -v www.michaelwlucas.com
Trying "www.michaelwlucas.com"
;; ->>HEADER<<- opcode: QUERY, status: NOERROR, id:
16073
;; flags: qr rd ra; QUERY: 1, ANSWER: 1, AUTHORITY: 0,
ADDITIONAL: 0

;; QUESTION SECTION:
;www.michaelwlucas.com.   IN   A

;; ANSWER SECTION:
www.michaelwlucas.com.   6904   IN   A   108.61.84.15

Received 55 bytes from 8.8.8.8#53 in 40 ms
```

You want detail, you got it!

Verbose output starts with the section HEADER and spills out general information about the DNS query and the response received. The important thing to note is the word NOERROR, which means that the DNS protocol worked.

In the QUESTION section we see that host specifically requested an A record.

Under ANSWER, the nameserver answered with an IP address.

At the very end we see the IP address of the nameserver host that was queried and how much traffic was received.

But wait, `host` isn't done yet! You'll see two similar searches as `host` queries for an AAAA and an MX record. No records of either of these types exist.

Let's consider something more complicated now: CNN's web site.[18]

```
# host www.cnn.com
www.cnn.com is an alias for www.cnn.com.vgtf.net.
www.cnn.com.vgtf.net is an alias for cnn-56m.gslb.vgtf.
net.
cnn-56m.gslb.vgtf.net has address 157.166.248.11
cnn-56m.gslb.vgtf.net has address 157.166.249.10
...
```

The first line shows that the host www.cnn.com is an alias for a host in another zone, www.cnn.com.vgtf.net.

The second line shows that www.cnn.com.vgtf.net is, in turn, an alias for yet another host. Two layers of redirection gives twice as many chances for something to blow up, but I don't have to run their site so I'm okay with this.

At the end we get the actual IP addresses for the site.

To perform a reverse DNS query, give `host` the IP address you want to get a hostname for.

```
# host 108.61.84.15
15.84.61.108.in-addr.arpa domain name pointer www.
michaelwlucas.com.
```

The output here is slightly different than you might expect. DNS is hierarchical, from right to left. IP addresses are also hierarchical, except the IP address hierarchy goes from left to right. Reverse DNS turns IP addresses around and puts them in the parent domain in-addr.arpa. (This is one of the few lingering traces of ARPANET, the Internet's predecessor.)

---

18   I'm demonstrating the Windows and Unix tools on the same zone because I want you to be able to compare the tools. It's not that I'm too lazy to go look for new examples. Really.

Despite the confusing output, it's pretty easy to see that the host 108.61.84.15 has reverse DNS pointing at www.michaelwlucas.com.

If you want to query a specific DNS server, give the hostname or IP of the DNS server after the host you want to query. Here I ask Google's backup nameserver what it knows about my web site.

```
# host www.michaelwlucas.com 8.8.4.4
```

You'll get the same sort of output as the default nameserver.

You can now query multiple recursive servers and see if the answers they give match. Differing answers probably mean that new DNS information is propagating across the Internet. Consistently wrong answers probably mean that an authoritative server has incorrect information.

Advanced DNS Queries

If you find that you want to get further into DNS, get a better tool. The two popular DNS toolkits are the Berkley Internet Name Daemon (BIND) and Unbound. Both are packaged for almost all modern operating systems and many obsolete ones. BIND includes the advanced query tool `dig`, while Unbound's advanced tool is called `unbound-host`.

If your operating system ships with one or the other, use it; but if you must choose something to install, go with BIND and `dig`. Either of these tools, along with various tutorials, will give you complete insight into DNS data.

The Hosts File

The Domain Name Service is not the only source of information on hostname-to-IP mappings. You can manually create these mappings

117

on an individual machine by using the hosts file. Unix uses the file
/etc/hosts, while Windows uses *C:\\Windows\System32\
drivers\etc\hosts*. Both files have the same format.

ipaddress   hostname aliases

To manually map the IP address 203.0.113.50 to the host storm.
mwlucas.org, make an entry like this.

```
203.0.113.50 storm.mwlucas.org
```

List any desired aliases after that entry.

```
203.0.113.50 storm.mwlucas.org windy rainy snowy
```

This machine can now find the host under any of those names.

I often put entries in my hosts file for troubleshooting. When I
develop a new version of my web site, I make a hosts entry for www.
michaelwlucas.com on my desktop, pointing to a development server.
This lets me verify that all of my links work and that I haven't done
anything actively stupid. Once my development work is complete, I
remove the hosts entry and push to production.

Lookups in the hosts file are much faster than querying a
nameserver. This is a valid reason for using a hosts file, especially if the
host repeatedly looks up a few select names. I would suggest that if the
few milliseconds needed for a DNS query is a problem, though, you
probably need to address a bottleneck somewhere.

Hosts Files Problems

The major problem with using a hosts file is removing old entries from
it—or, more specifically, not removing old entries. I've experienced
more than one outage caused by old entries in a hosts file. Be sure you
remove stuff that's no longer needed!

In large enterprises, I recommend using your configuration
management system (Ansible, Puppet, Chef, whatever) to maintain
production hosts files.

Name Resolution Order

Your systems can have multiple sources for hostname and IP information: DNS, the hosts file, possibly even LDAP or other local databases. When you ask the computer to find the IP address for a host, it checks each information source, in order, until it finds a match. The system takes the first answer. If your system checks the hosts file first, anything in the hosts file overrides DNS. If it checks DNS first, the hosts file is only checked when DNS doesn't have anything.

Many operating systems let you control where your system looks for host information and what order it checks those information sources in. Windows always checks the hosts file first. Most Unix systems use `/etc/nsswitch.conf` and/or `/etc/host.conf` to control which information source is checked first.

There's no textbook standard for which information source a system should use first. The important thing is that sysadmins know how a machine gathers information so she can use those information sources to her advantage.

Other Information Sources

A complicated network might have other sources of hostname to IP address mappings. Services like LDAP, YP, NIS, and more all include systems for providing IP addresses. Microsoft's WINS and NetBIOS will steer you to machines while leaving you kind of confused how you got there.

Disabling DNS

Some network services use DNS. Most of them do reverse DNS lookups on client IPs. Web servers might do a reverse DNS lookup on every client that visits the site. SSH servers can validate a client's reverse DNS before granting access. Network troubleshooting tools like `ping` and `traceroute` perform reverse DNS lookups on all the IP addresses they display.

These checks are very nice, when your recursive DNS server works quickly. When your DNS breaks, however, the service can collapse. One site I worked at had a widespread DNS service failure caused by insufficiently paranoid settings in the configuration management system. We pushed a broken nameserver configuration to all of our recursive servers simultaneously, breaking DNS everywhere, for everyone. (I highly recommend using a configuration management system like Ansible or Puppet—they let you deploy outages faster and with less effort.) The SSH service on the DNS servers performed reverse DNS lookups on SSH clients. The SSH daemons could not validate the client's reverse DNS, so nobody could log into the server to fix the problem!

Telling a service or daemon to depend on DNS to run adds another possible point of failure. Most Internet-facing services don't need to log the hostname of every client in real time. You can process those logs and add that information afterwards, without adding failure modes to your server.

When a service behaves badly and you just can't figure out what's wrong with it, try disabling any DNS dependencies. Your DNS might appear to be working fine, but there's a big difference between the one or two requests you run as a test and the thousands of requests per second that can come from a busy server. A few failed DNS requests can drag some server software to a crawl or make it entirely fail.[19]

Now that you can dazzle and annoy your DNS administrator with facts, let's see what traffic actually arrives at your server.

---

19   Should software be written such that it handles DNS failures gracefully? Of course. And in that world, I have a pony. No, wait—a unicorn. No, better still—a *ponycorn!*

Chapter 9: Packet Sniffing

The firewall administrator opened the port, but your server isn't getting any requests. Or you know traffic is leaving your web server because the access log shows the client request and the error log doesn't show a problem. Or desktops in the Outer Farawayistan office can ping your enterprise antivirus server, but none of them can register. What's going on?

A sysadmin trying to solve this kind of problem usually attacks every avenue simultaneously. She calls the vendor, who issues a ticket number and promises to ignore the matter at top priority. She calls the network team, who immediately says that the firewall is open and the problem is her server. She clicks random buttons and hopes. Eventually she starts studying H. P. Lovecraft, hoping that this Nyarlathotep dude can help her figure out what's going on.

One way to troubleshoot problems is to start lower down the network stack. Is the network traffic you expect arriving at your server? Is it leaving? You can try a `traceroute` (Chapter 12) to check for really bad network breakage, but a `traceroute` won't display subtle issues. That's where a packet sniffer comes in.

A *packet sniffer* displays packets as they cross a network interface. The sniffer can capture and display everything that arrives from the network and everything that leaves the server. Despite the language used to describe packet sniffing, sniffers don't actually create duplicates of the packets. Rather, they display information about packets and their contents. Packet sniffers have sophisticated filters that let you select exactly what traffic you capture and display, so you can narrow in on what you're looking for.

Suppose a client is having trouble accessing your service. Both you and the client have entered requests in your organizations to have all the firewalls and load balancers and packet filters and who *knows* what in between you configured to allow this access. The respective network teams have told you that everything is ready.

But the client can't access your service. You both check the obvious desktop settings and everything looks good. While you have the client on the phone, you fire up your packet sniffer and tell it to watch for the client's traffic.

If you don't see any traffic from the client, something is wrong somewhere on the network between the client and the server. This is where you open an issue with the network team and tell them that someone missed something. Maybe it's the client's network. Maybe it's yours. Who knows? But a trouble call that says "I'm not seeing any packets from my client" will receive more attention than a call that says "My app isn't working for this client."

If you see traffic from the client arriving at your server, but your server is not sending packets back to the client, you know it's something on your server. You can debug the problem yourself or call your vendor. Vendors are famous for answering every trouble call with "Check your firewall." Being able to say "I have verified that the traffic is reaching my server" will cut out a whole round of troubleshooting and help you prod them into action.

Can your client see the packets coming back to him? Maybe. He might lack the skills or system privileges to run a packet sniffer. But you know that you're sending him something, and that's valuable troubleshooting information for both network teams.

Either way, you've cut out several rounds of communication and dragged the problem's resolution much closer.

In certain high-security environments, you'll want to check with your manager before using a packet sniffer. Viewing certain kinds of traffic can cause legal issues in privacy-sensitive environments. Sensitive data should be encrypted as it goes over the wire, but ask before you get a surprise meeting with HR.

Packet Sniffers

Many operating systems include a packet sniffer or sniffer-like tools. Solaris has snoop. Microsoft has Network Analyzer. I focus on tcpdump and Wireshark.

Most packet sniffers have a good degree of interoperability. Wireshark, tcpdump, snoop, and just about everything else can read and write packet capture files the others can read. Which tool you use isn't as important as the information you gather.

tcpdump

Why tcpdump? It's been ported to every networked operating system. No matter what platform you run, you can get tcpdump.

The filtering language created for tcpdump, Berkeley Packet Filter (BPF) syntax, has become a standard part of networking. Almost every packet sniffer supports tcpdump-style BPF expressions, so your tcpdump education is portable.

Tcpdump is a small program. It runs in a text console, so it doesn't require any graphics libraries or programs. Tcpdump was written on machines that are smaller than any virtual machines you'll find today. It even fits easily on machines like the Raspberry Pi.

Unixes all either include `tcpdump` or have a `tcpdump` package. Some operating systems include an altered version of `tcpdump` that conforms more tightly to their platform's standards. This might include removing fields or changing default behavior. If the version of `tcpdump` shipped with your operating system deviates too much from what's here, look for a package of unmodified `tcpdump` or get it directly from http://www.tcpdump.org.

The most popular port of `tcpdump` for Windows is called `WinDump`. It's freely licensed for any use, commercial or non-commercial, and while it's based on an older `tcpdump` it's still quite serviceable. It requires the WinPcap library and drivers. Both `WinDump` and WinPcap are available from http://www.winpcap.org. Install WinPcap, and then `WinDump`. `WinDump` has made some changes to the output format—for example, the word Flags isn't shown before TCP flags, and commas are missing from a couple places. It still shows the information, it's merely not labeled the same. I'd whine about this, but everybody mucks with[20] `tcpdump`.

Everything that I say about `tcpdump` applies to `WinDump`. When I say `tcpdump`, I mean "`tcpdump` or `WinDump`."

One popular use for `tcpdump` is to capture traffic to a file, for analysis on a different machine. See "Capture Files" later this chapter.

Wireshark

While Wireshark is a newer, fancier packet sniffer, it's really a traffic analysis tool. Instead of a text console it has a graphic interface with buttons and click boxes. It can automatically decode many network protocols for you, reassemble complex data streams, and do it all in pretty colors.

---

20   One sysadmin's "improving" is another's "mucking with."

Wireshark is much larger than `tcpdump`. On Unix systems, it has a whole morass of dependencies on graphic libraries and such. Many sysadmins don't (and shouldn't) want all of that extra cruft on their servers.

Wireshark should *never* go on a production server. Always install Wireshark on a disposable virtual machine, for security reasons.

Packet Sniffer Security

All packet sniffers attach to a network interface at a low level. They need administrative privileges to run. This opens up interesting security issues.

Network defenders use packet sniffers to analyze data streams and identify malicious traffic. An intruder can create traffic specifically designed to exploit and corrupt packet sniffers. As packet sniffers run with administrative privilege, a corrupt packet sniffer could crash or damage the machine.

Modern operating systems run `tcpdump` in a sandbox to explicitly prevent this problem. `Tcpdump` exploit traffic is almost unknown outside the lab in any event.

Wireshark is a different story, however. It includes many protocol parsers, analyzers, and dissectors, all of which run with privileges. Malicious intruders have painstakingly created traffic streams specifically targeted at Wireshark's protocol parsers.

Do not run Wireshark on a production server. Ever. No, not even then.

If you need to use the pretty Wireshark GUI, use `tcpdump` (or one of the smaller, special-purpose Wireshark data capture tools) to copy the traffic you want to examine into a file. Copy the file to a disposable virtual machine. Use Wireshark on the virtual machine. You can then run Wireshark as a regular user, which should be much safer than running it with elevated privileges. If reading a traffic capture file with Wireshark destroys your VM, inform your organization's security officer.

Wireshark also supports remote streaming of sniffing traffic. You can run an agent on a server, and have the agent funnel traffic back to your Wireshark machine. This is a complex way to start packet sniffing, however. Don't try this until you're comfortable with `tcpdump` and ready to advance.

Packet Sniffer Interfaces

When you run a packet sniffer, you must decide which interface to sniff on, or *attach*. Many systems have only one physical network interface, but you might have multiple virtual interfaces and tunnels, not to mention the loopback interface. Some packet sniffers can capture traffic on USB ports or weird logical interfaces.

Each packet sniffer has a way to show you which interfaces you can sniff on. Choose the one you expect the traffic to appear on. You won't see many outside requests coming in over the loopback interface.

Encryption and Packet Sniffers

You've probably heard that FTP is bad because it sends passwords unencrypted over the network. You've heard that you should use SSH rather than telnet, for the same reason.

Packet sniffing proves this.

A packet sniffer can trivially capture usernames and passwords from unencrypted traffic. I'm not showing examples of this, as getting the recipe from your favorite search engine is also trivial. I'm sure that your network doesn't use unencrypted authentication protocols, anyway. You're a good person. You wouldn't support doing such things.

If you find yourself employed in an organization that uses unencrypted authentication, don't capture the boss' passwords as a demonstration and present them to the whole staff during a meeting. This goes over very poorly, and it seems that people take insecure protocols as a personal failure. It's much better to inform people that anyone *can* capture them, and then offer to demonstrate.

Using tcpdump

Before running `tcpdump` or `WinDump`, open a nice wide terminal window. If you're on Windows, use either PowerShell or Cygwin's mintty. `Tcpdump` generates wide output, and you'll have an easier time understanding it if each line doesn't wrap a bunch of times.

`Tcpdump` keeps reading from the network until you tell it to stop. On all platforms, use CTRL-C to terminate `tcpdump`.

Make sure you have administrative privileges before starting `tcpdump`. The easiest way to verify this is to check which interfaces `tcpdump` can sniff on.

Identifying Interfaces

To see which interfaces `tcpdump` thinks it can capture on, run `tcpdump -D`. Here's the output from a FreeBSD host.

```
# tcpdump -D
1.em0
2.lo0
```

Interface 1 is em0, and interface 2 is the loopback interface.

Windows lists the internal name for interfaces, showing the human friendly names at the end. Here's the output, run via PowerShell.

```
> .\WinDump.exe -D
1.\Device\NPF_{2D2767B0-D6BC-4142-8BC6-6DD1D2E13468} (Realtek PCIe GBE)
2.\Device\NPF_{B21F0FBF-8E9F-47C1-A557-4E2C57B238B2} (Microsoft)
3.\Device\NPF_{371F3AE1-D231-4500-8A87-AB1D2ED47353} (Microsoft)
```

Interfaces 2 and 3 are probably Microsoft internal things, but I recognize interface 1 as the network interface.

Whenever you need to specify an interface for `tcpdump`, you can use the number or the name. On Windows, I strongly encourage you to use the number.

Did `tcpdump` not display a list of interfaces? You probably don't have sufficiently high privileges for `tcpdump` to attach to the interfaces. Become root or Administrator and try again.

Specify an interface with `-i`, such as `-i em0` or `-i 1`.

```
# tcpdump -i 1
```

You can use an interface name from `ifconfig` as well as `tcpdump`'s interface number, if that's easier for you.

```
# tcpdump -i eth0
```

I'll go with the shorter interface numbers in my examples.

Your First tcpdump

Log onto a machine—any machine, even your desktop. Open a terminal window. Fire up `tcpdump` on your main network interface.

```
# PS C:\Program Files> .\WinDump.exe -i 1
C:\Program Files\WinDump.exe: listening on \Device\NPF_
    {2D2767B0-D6BC-4142-8BC6-6DD1D2E13468}
14:59:50.351940 IP snarkorama.michaelwlucas.com.62368
    > google-public-dns-a.google.com.53: 20011+PTR?
    255.255.255.255.in-addr.arpa. (46)
14:59:50.394999 IP google-public-dns-a.google.com.53 >
    snarkorama.michaelwlucas.com.62368: 20011 NXDomain
    0/1/0 (114)
...
```

Each line represents a single packet. And packets keep coming, flowing down your terminal window, in line after line of gibberish.

Terminate `tcpdump` with CTRL-C and you'll see something like this.

```
11 packets captured
74 packets received by filter
0 packets dropped by kernel
```

This last bit is easy enough to read. Tcpdump showed you 11 packets and received 74. The system didn't drop any packets during capture.

You probably think that this stuff looks utterly horrible. Packet captures aren't trivial to read, but compared to some of the SQL you server folks sling around it's a breeze. Let's take a few apart and see what they say.

Reading UDP Packets

Here's a line straight from the previous section.

```
14:59:50.351940 IP snarkorama.michaelwlucas.com.62368
   > google-public-dns-a.google.com.53: 20011+PTR?
   255.255.255.255.in-addr.arpa. (46)
```

The first field, 14:59:50.351940, is a timestamp. This packet was captured at 2:59 PM, according to the system clock, at 50.351940 seconds.

The second field, IP, shows that this is an IP packet. You'll see other protocols here, like IP6 for IPv6, or 802.1 for certain Ethernet management traffic.

The third field is the IP address or hostname that is the source of the packet. This packet came from the host snarkorama. michaelwlucas.com, the Windows laptop where I ran tcpdump. The source port, 62368, appears after the hostname or IP address, separated by a period.

The arrow indicates that this packet is moving on to another host.

The destination host is google-public-dns-a.google.com, on port 53. If you check the services file you'll see that port 53 is for DNS traffic.

If `tcpdump` understands the packet, it prints the packet contents at the end. Here we have DNS request number 20011, asking for the PTR record associated with the IP address 255.255.255.255.in-addr.arpa. Remember, PTR records and that in-addr.arpa stuff are parts of a reverse DNS query. This packet is a complete DNS request.

Last, we see that this query is 46 bytes.

That wasn't so bad, was it? Let's check out the second packet.

```
14:59:50.394999 IP google-public-dns-a.google.com.53 >
    snarkorama.michaelwlucas.com.62368: 20011 NXDomain
    0/1/0 (114)
```

This looks awfully similar to the previous packet. `Tcpdump` caught it at 2:59 PM, at 50.394999 seconds. This is 0.043059 seconds after the previous packet, an interval called "mighty quick" in any field except high-frequency trading. It's an IP packet from port 53 on Google's public DNS server, back to port 62368 on the client. It contains a DNS response. `Tcpdump` shows you that request 20011 gets an NXDOMAIN reply and a few DNS flags.

These two packets tell a very brief story. This machine did a DNS lookup and found that this host had no reverse DNS.

When I ran `tcpdump` here, I left DNS hostname lookups on. This meant that my client generates a whole bunch of DNS traffic, including lookups for the DNS servers themselves! This traffic overwhelmed other queries. I recommend always disabling DNS queries when running `tcpdump`, by using the −n flag. We'll see other ways to filter packet captures later this chapter.

Reading TCP Packets

Understanding TCP packets is more complicated than understanding UDP, because TCP itself is more complicated. A TCP packet shown in `tcpdump` resembles a UDP packet, but has additional information that represents the connection state and the packet's role in the data stream. You don't need to understand topics like sequence numbers or window scaling, but the Flags value is vital.

TCP Flags in tcpdump

The presence of a `Flags` value in a line of `tcpdump` output tells you that this is a TCP packet. TCP flags show the state of a connection. A TCP packet can and often should have multiple flags set. The flags are:

An *S* means that this is a SYN packet. It's part of the initial three-way handshake, either from the client or from the server.

A period (.) is an ACK, or an acknowledgement. This packet contains information acknowledging receipt of other packets.

An *R* is a TCP reset. The connection is forcibly terminated. If no connection exists yet, this translates to "connection refused." If it appears in the middle of an existing connection, a reset means "immediately throw away this connection, something has gone wrong."

An *F* in a FIN packet, part of the four-way connection teardown handshake. This connection is terminating gracefully.

You will see other flags, like *U* (urgent), *W* and *E* (for congestion control), or *P* (push). These flags are important for more complicated debugging, but their presence or absence won't affect the basic troubleshooting you're doing now.

Our First TCP Connection

Now let's `tcpdump` some TCP traffic. Here I'm running `tcpdump` on one of my servers. I've turned off name resolution.

```
# tcpdump -ni 1
16:19:24.326971 IP 203.0.113.50.39200 >
    108.61.84.26.80: Flags [S], seq 1660379222, win
    65535, options [mss 1460,nop,wscale 6,sackOK,TS
    val 2474478 ecr 0], length 0
```

The first five fields of a TCP packet are the same as a UDP packet. Each TCP packet starts with a very precise timestamp. This packet was seen at 16:19, or 4:19 PM, at 24.326971 seconds. The second field shows this is an IP packet.

Then we have the source address and port. This packet came from the host 203.0.113.50, on port 39200.

The arrow shows this packet was sent to the next host: 108.61.84.26, on port 80.

The Flags is where things get interesting. This packet contains one flag, S. It's a SYN packet. One SYN, all by itself, is the initial SYN request to open a TCP connection.

The following fields give packet sequence numbers, window size, and other options. These are integral to TCP, and of interest to network administrators, but you can't do much with them right now. Trust me, if something on your network shreds TCP sequence numbers, *everybody* knows the network has a problem!

Taken as a whole, this packet shows one host requesting a connection to port 80 on another host. Port 80 is for unencrypted web sites. This is probably the beginning of a HTTP request.

So let's look at the next packet.

```
16:19:24.376656 IP 108.61.84.26.80 >
   203.0.113.50.39200: Flags [R.], seq 0, ack
   1660379223, win 0, length 0
```

The timestamp says this is about a tenth of a second later. It's an IP packet, from port 80 on the host 108.61.84.26. It's going to the host 203.0.113.50, on port 39200. The previous packet was from the same hosts and ports, but in the opposite direction. This is a response to the first packet.

The flags are an R and a period (.). The R is a TCP reset. The period is an ACK, or acknowledgement.

Just as with our UDP trace, these two packets tell a little story. A client requests a connection. The server says "nobody here, go away."

I'm running `tcpdump` on the server, so I know that my server received this request and sent a response. Now you can start a more specific investigation. Does server have something—presumably a web server—listening to port 80? Is that process running? Is there a packet filter on my host that prevents the client from connecting to this port?

Without `tcpdump`, you'd have to pick up the phone and call the network team to see if they were blocking this traffic. And nobody wants you to do that.

TCP When Nobody Answers

You try to connect to a network service from your desktop and… nothing happens. Has the remote server process hung? Or is the client's traffic even reaching the other server?

When you connect to a network socket, the operating system kernel sets up the connection. Once it has a complete connection, it hands the incoming data stream to the server program. Say you have an SSH server listening on TCP port 22. The operating system knows that port 22 is open and attached to the SSH daemon. A request arrives for port 22. The operating system performs the TCP three-way handshake. Only when there's a working connection does the kernel poke the SSH daemon and say "Hey, this data stream is for you."

This helps determine where a problem lies. If a client can set up a three-way handshake, but never actually connects, it's probably the server program. If there is no three-way handshake, the operating system didn't complete the connection.

Here I try to connect to an SSH server and don't get an answer. Let's watch the network from the client and see what's going on. The client's IP address is 198.51.100.15. I've truncated the lines to remove the TCP options.

```
# tcpdump -ni 1
10:49:50.029434 IP 198.51.100.15.58381 >
    203.0.113.77.22: Flags [S], seq 3936280312, …
10:49:53.047102 IP 198.51.100.15.58381 >
    203.0.113.77.22: Flags [S], seq 3936280312, …
10:49:56.272359 IP 198.51.100.15.58381 >
    203.0.113.77.22: Flags [S], seq 3936280312, …
10:49:59.510151 IP 198.51.100.15.58381 >
    203.0.113.77.22: Flags [S], seq 3936280312, …
…
```

We've captured several packets. Look at the timestamps. They're all roughly three seconds apart. They're all IP packets, which is unsurprising.

But the source and destination addresses and ports are interesting. Every packet has the same source IP address, that of the client. They have the same destination address and port. What's more, the flags are the same on all of these packets. The only flag set is S, for synchronization request.

I've added one new field here, the seq or sequence number. TCP uses sequence numbers to indicate the order TCP packets go in. Sequence numbers are large random numbers. These sequence numbers are all the same, meaning that these are all the same packet, repeated over and over.

The client keeps resending the same synchronization request because the server isn't answering. The SSH server isn't trying to process my login request, it isn't answering at all.

If you have access to the SSH server through other means, you can check to see if it's receiving those packets.

Successful TCP

We've seen a couple of connections that don't work. Here I run `tcpdump` on a client that can connect to an SSH service. The client has the IP address 198.51.100.15, while the server is 203.0.113.26. Again, I've trimmed the TCP options and window size from the output to simplify study.

```
# tcpdump -ni 1
11:17:40.609154 IP 198.51.100.15.45439 >
    203.0.113.26.22: Flags [S], …
11:17:40.609886 IP 203.0.113.26.22 >
    198.51.100.15.45439: Flags [S.], …
11:17:40.609929 IP 198.51.100.15.45439 >
    203.0.113.26.22: Flags [.], …
11:17:40.611099 IP 198.51.100.15.45439 >
    203.0.113.26.22: Flags [P.], …
11:17:40.621635 IP 203.0.113.26.22 >
    198.51.100.15.45439: Flags [P.], …
…
```

Look at the timestamps first. These packets flew back and forth in just over a tenth of a second. Nothing here is timing out. We have packets going from the client's port 45439 to the server's port 22 and back.

Check out the flags, in order. The client sends a packet flagged with a SYN ("S"). The server responds with its own SYN and a period for an ACK ("."). The client returns an ACK, shown by the lone period. Data starts to flow back and forth, with ACKs and the PUSH ("P") flag.

Tcpdump isn't showing you the innards of this conversation, but you can see that the remote operating system has answered, set up a connection, and handed it off to a process. If your connection doesn't work, it's not a network issue. Something's gone astray with the server daemon.

Reading ARP

Reading TCP and UDP is useful, but sometimes watching the datalink layer is useful. Looking at ARP traffic can give insight into lower-level problems. Here's the Address Resolution Protocol in action.

```
# tcpdump -ni 1
11:35:48.468357 ARP, Request who-has 203.0.113.205 tell
    203.0.113.206, length 46
11:35:48.468377 ARP, Reply 203.0.113.205 is-at
    00:0c:29:4f:7d:91 (oui Unknown), length 28
```

As with all tcpdump entries, each packet starts with a timestamp. These two entries are hundreds of thousandths of a second apart.

The second field shows that these are not IP packets, but rather ARP frames. They run at the datalink layer, a level beneath TCP/IP.

The first frame is an ARP request. It's looking for the host 203.0.113.205. That host should send an answer to the host 203.0.113.206.

The second line is an ARP response, giving the physical (MAC) address that claims ownership of the IP address 203.0.113.205.

What if two different hosts respond to an ARP request, giving two different physical addresses for a single IP address? There's an IP address conflict. Neither host using this IP will be able to communicate reliably with other hosts on the network until the conflict is resolved.

ARP runs below IP, so it's not limited by IP subnet. If you have multiple IP networks on your Ethernet broadcast domain, as discussed in Chapter 3, `tcpdump` displays the ARP activity from all of them.

On more than one enterprise network, I've requested a new virtual machine and found that the network doesn't work. I can't ping the gateway or any other machines on my network. Logging in at the VM system console and running `tcpdump` shows that I see ARP traffic for a completely different subnet. A phone call that says "I can't ping the gateway" gets me a trouble ticket and a yawn. A phone call that says "I'm seeing ARP traffic from the production network on my dev box, and I can't see the dev network" gets a *much* faster response. Any network or cloud administrator who looks at that ticket will know immediately what the problem is and how to resolve it. You can also sniff the VM interface just to find out which network you're on before configuring the machine.

Other Traffic

Once you start looking at `tcpdump`, you'll discover all sorts of horrifying things on your network. In addition to IP and ARP traffic you'll uncover spanning tree announcements from network switches, network-booted devices searching for a configuration server, IPv6 on IPv4-only networks, and unspeakably weird crap. This tsunami of crap is normal, and almost impossible to eliminate from any network.

Unconvinced? Fire up `tcpdump` at home. Look at your own network. Try to figure out what all those things are and how to shut them up. A typical sysadmin has a home network with all kinds of devices on it: computers, switches, streaming media players, gaming consoles, coffeepots and ice cream sandwiches.[21]

Should someone track down all of these devices on your enterprise network and make them behave? Sure. But it's nearly impossible unless equipment and operating systems are purchased with "doesn't broadcast crap" at the top of the specification, in large unfriendly letters. Some enterprise equipment is specifically designed to broadcast weird crap, as part of a feature set nobody wanted in the first place.

Don't worry about small amounts of weird stuff on the network. You have enough real problems to worry about.

Filtering Captures

We've looked at individual packets captured by tcpdump, as well as short IP and ARP conversations. The problem is that servers don't exchange packets in neat little lists like that. A modern server can have tens of thousands of connections with thousands of clients simultaneously, processing millions of packets a second.

If you log into a remote server and run tcpdump, you'll get a whole bunch of output. Making it worse, every bit of tcpdump output travels across the network back to your client, creating more traffic, creating more output. Depending on how much traffic your server gets, this can create a death spiral.

What's more, much of that traffic won't interest you. If you're diagnosing a specific problem, you care about specific traffic. If one client can't access your server, you care about the traffic between your

---

21   No, not Android Ice Cream Sandwich. True sysadmins flash their desserts to the latest version before putting them in the freezer.

server and that specific client. All the other traffic is irrelevant. If you want to look at ARP traffic, you don't want to see any IP traffic.

`Tcpdump` has an extensive filtering language that lets you capture only the traffic that interests you. This filtering language, Berkeley Packet Filter or BPF, has become an industry standard by virtue of its flexibility and by being there first. The `tcpdump` manual has a complete description of the filtering language, but I'll discuss the most commonly used components and structures by example.

Why would you filter `tcpdump` captures, rather than filtering `tcpdump`'s output with `grep` or `findstr`? The more traffic `tcpdump` captures, the more system resources it consumes. Capturing all traffic on a busy server can conceivably cripple the machine. If you only capture the sliver of traffic you're interested in, `tcpdump` will use very few resources. On the other hand, you might need the entire haystack to find that troublesome needle.

Filter Format

`Tcpdump` filters use keywords and variables. You can combine keywords with logical operators like *and*, *not*, *or*, and parentheses. Filters go at the end of the command line, like so.

```
# tcpdump -n -i interface filter-expressions
```

The `-n` turns off DNS resolution. Specify an interface with `-i`. Add any other command-line flags you need, then put your filter expression.

I demonstrate logical operators throughout the following examples.

Capturing ARP Traffic

If you suspect that there's a duplicate IP on this network, or that the interface is attached to the entirely wrong network, you want to look at

Ethernet traffic. Use the `arp` keyword to view ARP transactions. Here I sniff ARP traffic on interface 1 (as enumerated by `tcpdump -D`), with DNS resolution off.

```
# tcpdump -ni 1 arp
```

This generates output like that in "Reading ARP" earlier this chapter.

You can filter by hardware address. A large or busy network might have lots of ARP traffic, and perhaps you're interested only in one particular host. Use the `ether host` keyword and a MAC address to filter `tcpdump` to only show traffic involving that MAC address.

```
# tcpdump -ni 1 ether host 9C:B6:54:1C:D4:E3
```

This shows only traffic to or from the MAC address 9C:B6:54:1C:D4:E3.

When you filter by MAC address you get everything from that hardware address. This includes ARP, TCP/IP, and whatever random strangeness that host is broadcasting. It's a great way to see if a host is broadcasting weird stuff, but perhaps you want to see only the ARP traffic for a specific host. Combine `ether host` with the `arp` keyword by using the AND logical operator.

```
# tcpdump -ni 1 arp and ether host 9C-B6-54-1C-D4-E3
```

AND requires satisfying both keywords. You'll see only ARP traffic, and only Ethernet traffic involving that MAC address. Combined, these two conditions greatly limit captured traffic.

Filtering by IP Addresses

Most commonly you'll be interested in TCP/IP traffic. To get rid of all the non-IP traffic, use the capture filter keyword `ip`.

```
# tcpdump -ni 1 ip
```

This will display all IP traffic. Even a server that seems mostly idle handles a surprising amount of IP traffic, so you probably want to trim this down further. The `ip host` keyword lets you filter by IP address. (Strictly speaking, this is two keywords. The `host` keyword tells `tcpdump` you're looking for a host, the `ip` means you're restricting this to IP traffic.)

```
# tcpdump -ni 1 ip host mail.michaelwlucas.com
```

I've used the -n flag to disable DNS lookups in the `tcpdump` output, but I can still use the target hostname in the filter. I could use the IP address on the command line if I preferred to.

Perhaps you're interested in multiple hosts. You might expect a database server to communicate with multiple web servers, and you want to see what's coming in from any of them. Use the `ip host` keyword and the OR logical operator. You don't need to use the keyword multiple times if you're repeating the same type of filter.

```
# tcpdump -ni 1 ip host 203.0.113.26 or 203.0.113.15
```

`Tcpdump` will print IP traffic that involves either of these IP addresses.

Perhaps your server has multiple IP addresses. You want to know about traffic exchanged between one of these addresses and a couple of other hosts. The traffic must involve your server's address, but it can have either client address. That's where parentheses come in.

Parentheses are a little complicated because you must use an escape character or quotes to keep your shell from interpreting them directly. Combine AND, OR, and parentheses to search out specific traffic. Here's a Unix `tcpdump` session where captured traffic must always include the host 203.0.113.64, and must always include one of the hosts 203.0.113.26 or 203.0.113.15.

```
# tcpdump -ni 1 ip host 203.0.113.64 and \(ip host
  203.0.113.26 or 203.0.113.15\)
```

On Unix systems put a backslash before either parenthesis, as shown above. Windows PowerShell uses a backtick (`) as an escape character, so the same filter in WinDump would look like this.

```
> ./WinDump -ni 1 ip host 203.0.113.64 and `(ip host
  203.0.113.26 or 203.0.113.15`)
```

You can also use single quotes around the entire filter to escape everything at once.

```
# tcpdump -ni 1 'ip host 203.0.113.64 and (ip host
  203.0.113.26 or 203.0.113.15)'
```

Maybe you're interested in traffic between your host and an entire network. Say the organization's database tier uses the IP range 192.0.2.0/24. Use the ip net keyword.

```
# tcpdump -ni 1 ip net 192.0.2.0/24
```

You must use the slash notation for a network, not a dotted-quad netmask like 255.255.255.0. On a Unix system you could use a network name from /etc/networks, but you have to configure that file and assign the network names yourself.

Perhaps you want to see everything on the traffic except a certain host or network. Bring in the NOT logical operator. You can use NOT all on its own, in front of any regular expression.

```
# tcpdump -ni 1 not ip host mail.michaelwlucas.com
```

If I excluded the NOT, this would mean "show everything going to or from my mail server." With the NOT, this shows all IP traffic that's going anywhere *except* to or from my mail server.

You could watch traffic exchanged with an entire network, except for a critical host.

```
# tcpdump -ni 1 ip net 192.0.2.0/24 and not ip host
    192.0.2.88
```

One item I'll commonly check is to see only traffic that leaves our local network.

```
# tcpdump -ni 1 ip and not ip net 192.0.2.0/24
```

Add in some parentheses and OR operators, and you can tune your capture filter exactly as you like. The AND and OR operators are not the typical Boolean priority, but prioritize from left to right. If you're not entirely sure what this means, group your filters with parentheses.

Capturing by TCP and UDP Ports

Limiting traffic by IP addresses helps, but you probably know what TCP/IP port you're interested in. If you manage a web server, ports 80 and 443 are of special interest. Mail uses 25 and 587, while client email services use ports like 110, 143, 993 and 995. By skipping traffic to any other ports, you can focus on exactly the traffic that interests you.

Use the protocol name as a keyword to filter on that protocol. Here I capture only UDP traffic.

```
# tcpdump -ni 1 udp
```

To focus on a specific port, use the `port` keyword.

```
# tcpdump -ni 1 tcp port 822
```

You can add the protocol without the AND keyword—that is, the filter `tcp port 22` is the same as `tcp and port 22`. If you want multiple ports, separate the keywords with AND and list your ports in parentheses. Here's a packet capture filter that our mail server administrator might use to check SMTP traffic.

```
# tcpdump -ni 1 tcp and \(port 25 or 587\)
```

You don't need to list the `port` keyword multiple times within one expression.

The most effective filters come when you can combine everything you know in a single filter. You're interested only in web traffic from a particular client? Fire up the sniffer on your server and write a filter to capture exactly that host. If our client is at 198.51.100.9, you could use a filter like this.

```
# tcpdump -i 1 ip host 198.51.100.9
    and \(tcp port 80 or 443\)
```

No matter how many clients are accessing this server at the moment you get your client to call up your web page, `tcpdump` displays only the traffic for this one IP address.

Capture Files

Maybe you want to look at a particular session of traffic more than once, or copy the traffic to a Wireshark workstation so you can use the pretty GUI. Maybe you have a weird problem with an application and want a network engineer to look at the traffic you're seeing, or you want to send a copy of the traffic to a vendor and say "See! This is what's causing my angina!" That's where a *capture file* comes in.

`Tcpdump` can copy all the packets it captures to a file. This isn't a copy of the screen's output—you can do that yourself with copy and paste—but, rather a binary dump of the actual packets. Read a capture file with `tcpdump`, another packet sniffer, or send it to an expert for detailed analysis.

Capture files can contain sensitive information. Any authentication information that's sent unencrypted will appear in plain text inside the capture file. It's binary-encoded, yes, but it's plain text to anyone who can run `hexdump` or `tcpdump -vv`. Wireshark will happily decode most plain text passwords. Don't go sending a packet capture of a complete telnet or FTP session to your vendor for troubleshooting, as anyone can read your authentication information from the file.

Capturing to a File

Specify a capture file with −w and the file name. Traditionally, capture files end in .pcap. Capturing packets in tcpdump doesn't generate any output. Add the −v flag to constantly display how many bytes you've captured, so you can tell if you've captured anything.

Here I capture web traffic (ports 80 and 443) between my Windows client and a host named www. Rather than displaying the packets, I save the traffic to a capture file named web.pcap.

```
> ./WinDump -w web.pcap -ni 1 ip host www
  and `(port 80 or 443`)
```

Tcpdump (or WinDump, in this case) won't print any packets. It writes the contents to the file instead. Reproduce the issue, giving tcpdump some packets to write. Hit CTRL-C to end tcpdump. This closes your capture file and lets you analyze it.

When you're trying to figure out a problem, I recommend writing generous filters. If I'm having trouble with my server and I want to use a capture file, I probably wouldn't filter on ports, but only on IP addresses. I might want to do more analysis on that packet capture later and look for weird things.

Some people prefer not filtering capture files at all. They capture all the data received while the problem is going on, and then filter it later during analysis. They don't risk losing relevant information to a capture filter.

Capture files can grow very large very quickly. Don't start a tcpdump capture and go to lunch. You might return to find your disk full and the machine wedged.

Reading a Capture File

Want to read a capture file in `tcpdump`? Use the `-r` flag.

```
# tcpdump -r web.pcap
```

You can re-run `tcpdump` filters against a capture file. If you want to disable DNS lookups in the output, add the `-n` flag.

```
# tcpdump -nr web.pcap
```

Perhaps you want to see only port 80 traffic in this capture file. Add a filter for that port at the end.

```
# tcpdump -nr web.pcap port 80
```

Maybe you want to see everything the client sent except web traffic.

```
# tcpdump -nr web.pcap not \(port 80 or 443\)
```

You can also open capture files in Wireshark for more detailed examination.

Capture files let you look at the same connection over and over, any way you can imagine. Let's quit looking at traffic we're passively receiving, though, and make and receive our own packets on demand.

Chapter 10: Creating Traffic

Nobody likes reproducing the problem. Even if you personally created the problem, and you think you know exactly how it happened, myriad factors can prevent your tools from failing in exactly the same way. Reproducing a problem is always a struggle.

Changing network conditions complicate problem replication. If email isn't flowing, and you don't see email packets arriving at your server, suspecting the network is reasonable. The problem might be the software that's supposed to generate the traffic. You need the ability to validate network connectivity without any complicated client/server software in the middle.

That's where `netcat` comes in. `Netcat` lets you generate arbitrary TCP/IP traffic. You want to know if a client can connect to TCP ports 25 and 587 on your mail server? Stop using your email program to generate traffic. Fire up `netcat` on your client, point it at those ports on the server, and see if the packets arrive.

`Netcat` can also create arbitrary sockets and report on the data that arrives at them. Say you need to install a new web server instance. You encounter the firewall administrator in the break room at two in the morning, when you're both rummaging through other people's abandoned lunches looking for something to tide you over until the Problem of Doom is solved and everyone can go home. She tells you that the firewall should be open, but to enter a trouble ticket if you have a problem.

Entering and resolving trouble tickets takes much more time than installing and configuring any piece of familiar software. Before you even start trying to install the software, run a `netcat` command to create sockets on port 80 and 443. See if you can send traffic to and from them. If you find a network issue, open the firewall change request before you kick off the installation job. (Always start the slowest part of any process first, and work on the quicker tasks while you wait for the slow task to finish.)

If you need to test HTTP-based connectivity, you can generate traffic with a web browser or a program like `wget`, `curl`, or `fetch`, whatever your operating system includes.

Often you'll hear advice to test whether a port is open with the telnet client. Telnet for network testing is terribly limited. Telnet only works on TCP ports, while `netcat` lets you send and receive both TCP and UDP traffic. Telnet is also a client program designed for a specific purpose. Some of those client functions, like error messages, can confuse simple network tests. Telnet works, except when it doesn't, and except when you think it should.

Your average network administrator knows about the problems with using telnet to test connectivity, and experience will lead her to dismiss telnet-based-test failures. If telnet reports that the network is open, it probably is. If it reports the network is closed, it might not be.

Netcat and Security

`Netcat` has been called a networking Swiss Army Knife. It lets you slice, dice, and interconnect network ports any way you want. `Netcat` is not a security tool, but it is used by security professionals. If you can use a tool to test if a port is open, an intruder can use that tool for the same purpose.

148

When you use a broadly useful tool like `netcat`, be sensitive to your environment's security policy. Some high-security organizations even ban specific programs on servers because of their potential for abuse. If you work in one of those organizations, you have no choice but to get the network team to check things for you.

Which Netcat

`Netcat` came out in 1995 and shows its age by, among other things, lacking IPv6 support. `Netcat` has been forked, rewritten, extended, and improved by many people since its release. Today, most Unixes use a version of `netcat` from the OpenBSD project, which added IPv6.

Some Unix systems (most notably Debian Linux) ship with original `netcat`. You'll need to install the netcat-openbsd package to get IPv6 support. CentOS Linux includes a modern `netcat` in the nmap-ncat package.

Windows doesn't include `netcat`, but many people have ported `netcat` to Windows. I usually use Jon Craton's Netcat for Windows port, available at your favorite search engine. Sphinx Software has a Windows Netcat version for IPv6. Both of these are command-line versions, but several people have written graphic front ends. Look around and choose one you like.

You can also find tools where someone took the ideas behind `netcat` and built a more powerful TCP/IP connection toolkit. Socat and Nmap's `ncat` are two big candidates here. These advanced features incur complexity and often expect you to have more TCP/IP knowledge than you need. I recommend `netcat` here specifically because it's simple. `Netcat` lets you perform basic connectivity tests without a lot of system overhead or wasting your precious brain capacity.

Connecting with Netcat

The most common use of `netcat` is to connect to a TCP or UDP port.

Connecting with TCP

`Netcat` defaults to using TCP. For a TCP connection give it two arguments, the hostname or IP and the port number. Here I connect to my web server on port 80. Add the `-v` to display errors, as discussed in "Netcat Errors" later this chapter.

```
# nc -v www.michaelwlucas.com 80
www.michaelwlucas.com [108.61.84.15] 80 (http) open
```

If the client establishes a TCP session, you'll get a blank new line. `Netcat` hasn't sent any application data, but it has performed the TCP three-way handshake. I'm connected directly to whatever service is listening on the other side.

If I'm really connected to a web server, I should be able to enter HTTP requests by hand and get an answer. I type:

```
GET / HTTP/1.1
host: www.michaelwlucas.com
```

I hit ENTER twice at the end, as per the HTTP protocol specification. The web server returns the text of a HTTP response, redirecting me to the SSL version of my web page.

My `netcat` connection remains open for a couple of seconds, then the server closes it. To forcibly close the connection, enter CTRL-C.

If I can grab the page source with `netcat` but it won't display in my browser, then something's amiss in the application layer.

Connecting with UDP

To create a UDP connection with netcat, add the -u flag. Here I see if I can transmit UDP packets from my client to a particular server's DNS port.

```
# nc -uv dns1.mwl.io 53
```

Again, I get a blank line. Type some things to send data to that port.

Netcat plays fast and loose with UDP's connectionless nature. Strictly speaking, a UDP packet is a complete entity in and of itself. UDP doesn't imply an answer. The fact that you're running something over UDP kind of implies that you expect some sort of response, however. Netcat listens for a response from the server, and if it sees one it prints it to the terminal. To end the netcat session, hit CTRL-C.

Manual testing of UDP-based protocols is difficult. Many protocols that run on TCP, like HTTP and SMTP, are designed around a back-and-forth exchange of text. You can enter the protocol commands by hand and get the server software on the other end to respond. A UDP protocol, like much of DNS, has no concept of connections. A program can send something over UDP. Something might come back. Or not. Netcat lets you verify that the transport layer works, however.

Netcat Errors

Suppose the remote host doesn't answer?

Netcat doesn't normally send its own error messages amidst the data exchanged with the server. It puts those debugging details on standard error rather than standard out. To display the error messages, add the -v flag as I've done in the previous examples.

If you omit the −v, you won't get any error messages at all. If the netcat client receives an answer that says "This port is not open," such as a TCP reset or the "port unreachable" ICMP messages used for UDP, netcat immediately returns a command prompt.

If no answer comes back, then netcat hasn't received an answer from the remote host. There hasn't been a TCP reset or a port unreachable message. This is no different than trying to connect to a non-responsive host with any other client.

```
# nc -v mail.mwl.io 80
nc: connect to mail port 80 (tcp) failed: Connection
refused
```

My mail server doesn't run a web server, so it rightly refuses the connections.

Errors from attempted UDP connections tend to be less informative, as there's no requirement to return any error from an ignored UDP packet. Some secure networks filter out error messages from UDP specifically to dissuade intruders.

Listening with Netcat

You can use tcpdump to see traffic arrive at a host, or application logs to see that someone's poking at your server. Netcat can act as a mini-server, letting you create *netcat listeners* on arbitrary TCP/IP ports. With a netcat listener on one host, and netcat on another, you can send data, files, or anything from one host to another across any TCP/IP port.

TCP listeners

Use the −l flag to tell netcat to listen. Netcat uses TCP by default, so to listen on a TCP port give the port number. Here I show how you can create a network socket on TCP port 9999 on a server at 203.0.113.50.

```
# nc -l 9999
```

You won't get a prompt back: the command just hangs there.

Open a terminal prompt on another machine. Use `netcat` to connect to the server on TCP port 9999.

```
# nc 203.0.113.50 9999
```

You still won't get a command prompt back; `netcat` is waiting for input.

Type something in your `netcat` client window. Once you hit RETURN, the text appears in the server's `netcat` session. Anything typed on the server side appears in the client's session. You can go back and forth as much as you want.

To terminate the listener, hit CTRL-C in either `netcat` session.

Testing traffic back and forth with `netcat` validates that you have a functional network connection between these two hosts.

UDP Listeners

While TCP has all that nifty error correction, you can also build a UDP tunnel. Use the -u flag when creating your listener. Here's a `netcat` listener on UDP port 8888 on a server at 203.0.113.50.

```
# nc -ul 8888
```

Again, you get a blank line instead of your command prompt.

Go to your client and tell `netcat` to make a UDP connection to the server on port 8888.

```
# nc -u 203.0.113.50 8888
```

Type in one window. The output appears in another.

UDP lacks TCP's error correction. On a lossy or slow network you might lose some data from the exchange. Netcat doesn't implement any error correction—it gives you low-level access directly to network ports, rather than covering up lower-layer weirdness. Netcat displays exactly what it receives. Real applications that use UDP implement their own error correction.

Sending Files With Netcat

Always use approved methods to copy files from one machine to another. Do not bypass your organization's standards just because you can. Every organization has ways it wants you to send files around the network. Avoiding them can result in a pointed, perhaps even downright cranky session with the corporate security officer. In a disaster, however, you can use netcat to send a file from one host to another. Netcat has no encryption, so don't send sensitive data over it.

Create a listener on the destination machine. Redirect the output to a file. I recommend using TCP so that the network protocol will correct for any transmission errors.

```
# nc -l 9999 > received_file
```

The contents of any data stream sent to TCP port 9999 will get sent to the specified file.

Sending the file itself is somewhat more complicated. You need to tell the netcat client to close after it finishes the file. Use the -N flag on OpenBSD-derived netcats. On Debian-based systems, use -q 0. Here I send a file from a Debian system to port 9999 on my server at 203.0.113.205.

```
# nc -q 0 203.0.113.205 9999 < testfile
```

When the file is completely sent, the netcat client shuts itself off.

Again, this isn't for routine use. But when you find yourself trying to get a machine out of single-user mode and can't get a functional kernel on it any other way, copying files with netcat is a good trick to pull out of your toolbox.

More Netcat Fun

A little research uncovers all sorts of fun things you can do with
`netcat`. You can attach a command shell, privileged or not, to a
`netcat` listener, or send files from your `netcat` listener straight into
a decompression program. You can capture UDP queries, like DNS,
and replay them for debugging purposes. I advise extreme caution
in using these functions on an organization's network, however.
Specifically, you'll see lots of examples of attaching a command shell to
a TCP/IP port. Anyone who happens to connect to that port will get
shell access. This makes the security people nervous. There's no point
in learning all this TCP/IP stuff and improving your relationship with
the network crew only to turn around and distress the security folks.

Speaking of security, why should the firewall and router teams
have all the filtering fun? You can implement packet filters on your
own servers.

Chapter 11: Server Packet Filtering

Packet filtering is a tool for prohibiting access to TCP/IP ports and/or IP addresses. It's often considered the province of network and firewall administrators, but it's a valuable tool on servers as well.

Most operating systems, from big servers to cell phones, can filter network traffic. The feature is frequently called a firewall, but the word firewall has been so badly stretched and abused it means nothing. Operating systems use packet filters similar to those found on routers and hardware firewalls. They use antivirus software and other security controls for proxy-like functions. This chapter doesn't cover the specifics of configuring any individual vendor's packet filter, but focuses on when and why you might consider using packet filters on your hosts.

To understand when you'd want packet filtering on a server, first consider how an intruder can attack your network.

Network Intrusions

People responsible for network security often get called "paranoid." It's as though they feel that the whole world is out to get them. Unfortunately, this feeling has a very real basis in fact. Some intruders target very specific organizations, while others want to get administrative access to every single machine they can get their grubby hands on.

Even if your organization has absolutely no valuable, confidential, or unique data, your processing power is valuable. Intruders have hijacked machines to install Bitcoin miners or Internet chat robots. These processes can destroy data, cause performance problems, and trigger outages. A security team's job is to prevent these incidents.

Packet filtering is part of a security strategy. An intruder can't compromise a machine they cannot directly or indirectly interact with. The goals of network security can be summed up in the five Ds of physical security: deter, detect, deny, delay, and defend. Let's look at this from both an enterprise perspective and an individual perspective.

Organizational Intruders

Consider a typical global enterprise network. It has routers to connect it to the Internet. Inside the routers it has border firewalls. There's a low-security network where they keep public-facing applications. There's a high-security zone where their private data lies. Then there's the desktop arena, where the most vulnerable and dangerous computers live.

The security team implements controls at each layer of the network. At the Internet routers they use packet filters that prevent private IP addresses from leaving the network and only allow specific inbound traffic. These routers must permit external clients to access the public-facing web servers, because those web servers are part of the reason they have an Internet connection.

The border firewall implements more specific protections. Certain web servers are open to the public, while others are only open to specific business partners. The firewall sanity-checks every web request before handing it to the web servers.

Nothing from the outside world can access the database or the desktop networks. The web servers can query the database servers that support their applications.

Now imagine an intruder who wants to extract information from the databases. He needs to discover a path to get instructions to the databases. Each layer of filtering and proxying deters or denies him. Slithering malicious commands through the narrow gaps in the defenses delays him. Every action the intruder takes increases the odds of detection.

Say your intruder gets unprivileged access to the database servers. As the system administrator, the defense of the network is now in your hands. A slick and savvy intruder might evade your notice as well, but you have an advantage: the intruder will almost certainly change something on your server. If he dumps and compresses a copy of your database, disk usage will jump. He might install a piece of software. I've seen intruders create system accounts for themselves, install their favorite text editor, and load their preferred shell resource files containing their favorite command aliases.

Every change an intruder makes increases the odds of detection. If you don't notice the surge in disk usage, maybe you'll notice the new accounts, or the new software installation, or the mysterious reboot. Hopefully the organization's intrusion detection system or routine network analysis will pick up some of this activity.

Packet filtering plays into a security strategy by denying access to an intruder, forcing him to explore other options. It also can compel the intruder to change the system to achieve his goals.

Single Server Intruders

At the other extreme, you have people like me. I have a small web server and a personal mail server. Nobody is going to hack my web server to get early copies of my books, but someone will take my disk space, processor time, and bandwidth for their Bitcoin mine if they can. Having my servers hacked is bad enough, but then having to pay a hosting provider for it just twists the kukri.

Will packet filtering help? Maybe. I know exactly what services should come into my hosts. I know exactly what traffic should leave my hosts. Using a packet filter on the servers might well deter, deny, or delay an intruder. Once an intruder gets user-level access, permitting only narrow outbound access will certainly frustrate him.

If the intruder gets administrative access, he can disable packet filtering. But if an intruder cracks administrative access, the packet filter is the least of your problems. And again, the change to the system increases the chances you'll notice the intrusion.

Server Packet Filtering

If you decide to filter traffic at the server, the first thing to remember is that you don't know what traffic your server needs to perform its work. You only think you know. Start working with server-side packet filtering in a development or test environment before going anywhere near production.

Packet filtering on the server usually takes two forms: inbound and outbound.

Filtering Inbound Traffic

Each open TCP/IP port on a host offers possible ways for an attacker to penetrate the host. Your server probably runs a whole bunch of services, and has lots of open TCP/IP ports (see Chapter 6 to check yours).

Should the firewall protect these ports on your host? Yes… and no.

Look at our example organization in the previous section. An intruder might break into a web server and use that as his forward base for further intrusions. He can only run limited SQL queries against your databases, but what else does the web server have access to? He might jump from the web server into the machine that runs backups. (You do back up all your machines, don't you?) From the backup machine, he might hop straight into your database server.

If each open TCP/IP port on your server is a potential avenue of attack, treat it as such. The backup controller might need access to the client running on the server, but it probably doesn't need file sharing or Windows RPC or SSH or web access. Block all those things. Reduce the important server's exposure to potential threats.

Your server probably runs all kinds of services used only by the local host, and it probably offers all of them on its network interface. Why should other hosts be able to access them? Block that stuff. Block everything except what the server specifically provides.

By blocking all traffic by default, only permitting access to traffic that the server needs to fulfill its role, you narrow an intruder's options. You deny, deter, and delay his work, making detection and defense much more likely.

Filtering Outbound Traffic

Filtering traffic generated by a server is more difficult only because most sysadmins have no idea what traffic their server needs to perform its role. While developing rules for outbound packet filtering can be vastly annoying, it will annoy the intruder even more.

An intruder who wants to install an IRC bot, a Bitcoin miner, or a botnet client on your server will find that your server cannot communicate with the other infected machines in the attacker's network. The intruder who wants to exfiltrate data from the server will find getting the data off the server almost as annoying as getting into the server in the first place. Yes, he could use a `netcat` tunnel to copy the data around the network in a series of successive hops—once he figures out which hosts he can communicate with, and on which ports. If he gets administrative access he could change the host's firewall rules. But every change an intruder makes increases the odds of you detecting him.

Outbound packet filtering works best in environments with strong central services. If you have a central proxy server, the clients don't need outbound web or FTP access. If they get patches from a central server, they don't need access to the vendor's hosts. And why would they need to browse the desktop network? If the intruder must funnel his outbound database dump through a proxy server with tight access controls and filtering, or tunnel his SSH upload into DNS queries, the odds of detection increase dramatically.

If you're in an environment where you create and destroy virtual machines through an automation system such as Ansible or Puppet, you have a well-defined network. There's no reason to not filter outbound traffic on all hosts in these environments.

I advise blocking all outbound access. Permit only what the server needs to perform its functions. Even if nobody breaks in, by filtering outbound access you'll learn more about how the server's applications actually function.

Packet Filtering Configurations

Some packet filters can be dynamically adjusted on the fly. Applications can even add their own filter rules if you allow it. I encourage you to disable these features except for very narrow uses. If your applications can change packet filtering rules, so can the intruder's applications. Applications that change the filtering rules tend to do so promiscuously, permitting the whole world to access them instead of the desired clients.

Put your packet filter rules in a configuration file that the operating system cannot change. Load those rules at boot time. Consider and evaluate changes before deploying them.

While you're at it, be sure to protect, secure, and verify access to your system console. Most systems, both virtual and physical, come with some sort of remote console. Be sure that when you break your Remote Desktop Server or SSH daemon, you can get in with a keyboard.

Now that you've protected your domain, let's explore things that are definitely other people's problems: the external network.

Chapter 12: Tracing Problems

The Internet is a network of interconnected networks. To communicate with another host, a host must send traffic through these interconnects. Packets wend their way from host to host, being interpreted and inspected and repeated at each hop, until they reach their destination. If something fails along the way, the communication fails.

The `traceroute` program lets you follow packets as they travel between hosts, viewing what hosts they pass through to reach their destination. It's a highly valuable tool, but it's also badly misunderstood. Using `traceroute` and correctly interpreting the results can narrow down network problems.

Most operating systems ship with `traceroute`. Microsoft Windows calls it `tracert`. If your operating system doesn't include `traceroute`, it has an optional package for it.

`Traceroute` has been re-implemented multiple times as people have added their own twists to the program. For our purpose, any version suffices—you won't use the advanced features that come in some of the more complex `traceroute` utilities.

Whenever you use a diagnostic tool like ping or `traceroute`, note the clock time you run the command. Timing is very important in diagnosing and resolving network issues. I have had more than one issue that happened only at specific times, such as "every hour at 16 minutes past the hour" or, worse, "every 16 minutes and 40 seconds." Timestamps help narrow down those most annoying intermittent problems.

Chapter 12: Tracing Problems

The best way to use `traceroute` is if you know the path the traffic should take. Run some traceroutes to sites you normally interact with. Note what those traces look like. Preferably, copy them into a file somewhere. When you get a problem report, run a new `traceroute` and compare it to the known working `traceroute`. Traffic suddenly taking a new route might just be the problem.

Our First Traceroute

To run `traceroute` give it one argument: the destination server.

Some `traceroute` versions give slightly different output—notably, they put the host or IP before the timestamps. They all include the same general information, however. Here's a `traceroute` from a private network to my web server.

```
# traceroute www.michaelwlucas.com
Tracing route to www.michaelwlucas.com [108.61.84.15] with TTL of 32:

1 0ms 0ms 0ms 67.210.17.1
2 0ms 0ms 1ms gi0-8.na21.b006097-0.mia01.atlas.cogentco.com
    [38.100.206.113]
3 2ms 1ms 1ms 154.24.28.238
4 3ms 1ms 1ms te0-0-0-1.agr12.mia01.atlas.cogentco.com [154.24.10.73]
5 2ms 1ms 1ms te0-4-1-0.ccr21.mia01.atlas.cogentco.com [66.28.4.217]
6 1ms 1ms 1ms 154.54.80.42
7 1ms 1ms 1ms xo.ord03.atlas.cogentco.com [154.54.12.230]
8 * 34ms 34ms xe-4-0-1.nyc39.ip4.gtt.net [141.136.110.158]
9 34ms 34ms 34ms gtt-gw.ip4.gtt.net [173.241.131.238]
10 39ms 35ms 39ms as20473.ae7.ar1.nyc3.us.as4436.gtt.net [69.31.34.62]
11 35ms 35ms 35ms 108.61.244.41
12 35ms 35ms * ethernet1-49-cl1-8-c6-1.pnj1.choopa.net [108.61.138.62]
13 35ms 35ms 35ms www.michaelwlucas.com [108.61.84.15]


Traceroute complete.
```

`Traceroute` starts by repeating its target's hostname and IP address. If you're having trouble with one of your servers, this line can alert you to DNS problems.

Each following line is a separate host (router or router-like device, such as a firewall) along the way. The number at the start of the line is the hop number.

You'll then get three timestamps, one for each packet sent to that hop. Where a single packet might get lost, sending three packets gives a good chance of something getting through. The time stamp is how long it takes for a packet to reach that hop and return. It's a round-trip time, not a one-way trip. Each time stamp is its own packet. Our first hop needs zero milliseconds to get to the next router and back. It's not literally zero, but the time is so small that it doesn't round off to even a single millisecond. It's fast. Conversely, at the last hop, each packet needs 35 milliseconds to reach my web server and return. That's still pretty quick.

We then have the host at each hop. It usually appears as the hostname (if present in reverse DNS), then the IP address of the host.

So what can we learn from this?

Look at hops 7 and 8. Hop 7 takes one millisecond. At hop 8, we have an asterisk and two 34-millisecond times. What's going on? The asterisk indicates a lost packet. Either the request did not reach the device, this device did not respond to this packet, or the response did not make it back to the client. But take a look at the hostnames. Hop 7 is in the domain cogentco.com, while hop 8 is in gtt.net. These are both Internet *backbone carriers*, really big long-distance Internet Service Providers. We cross between carriers at this point. It's common for times to increase at these interconnection points. Different backbones have different traffic policies and practices.

What about the asterisk, the missing packet? That isn't cause for concern. Let's talk about some common errors you'll see.

Traceroute Errors

Traceroute can expose a lot of problems. Some of them might even be real network issues. Let's consider some of the common headaches.

Slow Traces

Traceroute might run very, very slowly. A common cause of this is DNS lookups. Traceroute does a reverse DNS check of every hop along the way. If you have weird problems and traceroute runs slowly, verify your DNS servers work.

If traceroute runs quickly without DNS, but slowly with DNS, look very hard at your DNS services. Disable DNS lookups with -n (Unix) or -d (Windows).

"starring out"

An asterisk in a timestamp means a dropped packet. A single dropped packet at an intermediate hop means nothing. But what happens when your traceroute ends in a bunch of asterisks, appearing one every two seconds or so?

If the traceroute couldn't find a way to send the packets on, or if an interface was down you'd get a specific error, probably one of the exclamation point errors discussed later. An asterisk means that the previous host forwarded a packet, but that no response came back to your client. Traceroute can't print a hostname or IP for the troubled hop, because there's no information about it. If no packets come back, the only thing traceroute can do is shrug and say "I dunno, here's an asterisk."

This might mean that the remote host can't reply to you (see "Asymmetric Routing" later this chapter). It might also mean that the next hop filters the UDP or ICMP traffic used for traceroute. This is very common for security-sensitive organizations. A `traceroute` to your bank's web site probably ends in a stream of asterisks.

Always let a `traceroute` run for a couple of lines of asterisks before canceling it. Sometimes a single host along the path doesn't respond to `traceroute` requests, but hosts beyond it do. Here's a slice of a `traceroute`.

```
...
5  76-73-165-86.knology.net (76.73.165.86)  22.342 ms  35.650 ms
   22.281 ms
6  * * *
7  unknown.prolexic.com (209.200.144.161)  29.007 ms  54.267 ms
   28.522 ms
...
```

Each of those three asterisks took two seconds to appear. That feels like an awful long time when you're staring at the terminal. If I had canceled the `traceroute` before letting line 6 finish, I never would have seen hop 7 and later.

Multiple lines of asterisks usually mean that you cannot `traceroute` beyond this point, but a single line means that one host along the way isn't answering your `traceroute`. You might try from a public `traceroute` server, discussed later this chapter.

You might find that your home connection drops a lot of `traceroute` packets. Some ISPs filter or rate-limit `traceroute` traffic. If you can't get a better service provider, you might have to rely on public `traceroute` servers.

Time Spikes

Sometimes you'll see a hop with very high times compared to the hosts around it.

Routers are designed to forward traffic. Responding to traffic addressed to the router itself takes more effort than forwarding traffic. Routers respond to traceroutes and pings at a low priority. If a router is even vaguely sorta busy, it delays or defers responding to `traceroute` requests.

If a particular hop loses packets or has high response times, but the following hops look better, the router with the high times has decided to not spend any energy processing your `traceroute` request. This is very common on busy network interconnects. The really big networks in your country exchange a lot of traffic, and those routers get a lot of these requests because of their critical placement.

Time Jumps

Timestamps might get really high at a certain hop, and remain high at all following hops. At first guess it seems that a network runs really poorly at a particular point, which implies a problem. For example, here's a `traceroute` to a friend's web site from my home in Detroit.

```
# traceroute phk.freebsd.dk
traceroute to phk.freebsd.dk (130.225.244.222), 64 hops max, 52 byte
packets
 1   203.0.113.1 (203.0.113.1)  1.280 ms   1.136 ms   1.544 ms
 2   69-19-191-33.static.try.wideopenwest.com (69.19.191.33)   11.900 ms
     10.542 ms   10.738 ms
 3   dynamic-76-73-172-53.knology.net (76.73.172.53)   9.603 ms
     10.487 ms   10.171 ms
 4   76-73-165-186.knology.net (76.73.165.186)   21.146 ms   12.257 ms
     13.267 ms
 5   76-73-164-89.knology.net (76.73.164.89)   22.101 ms   20.040 ms
     21.109 ms
 6   76-73-164-65.knology.net (76.73.164.65)   25.698 ms   25.768 ms
     21.511 ms
 7   static-76-73-191-224.knology.net (76.73.191.224)   24.847 ms
     23.289 ms   22.070 ms
 8   user-75-76-127-229.knology.net (75.76.127.229)   22.564 ms
     23.127 ms   19.532 ms
 9   xe-10-1-1.chi11.ip4.gtt.net (77.67.77.109)   22.225 ms   24.989 ms
     20.750 ms
10   xe-0-0-0.cph10.ip4.gtt.net (89.149.187.30)   124.556 ms   122.035 ms
     122.027 ms
11   te-dix.ly0.core.fsknet.dk (192.38.7.1)   141.447 ms   154.949 ms   ·
     122.832 ms
```

```
12  10g-ly0.ly3.core.fsknet.dk (130.226.249.190)  126.465 ms
    126.849 ms  126.685 ms
13  phk.freebsd.dk (130.225.244.222)  127.631 ms  123.800 ms
    126.212 ms
```

Hop 9 has a 22 millisecond round trip time. Hop 10 jumps by 100 milliseconds, and that lag stays around throughout the rest of the `traceroute`. Obviously something's running slowly between these hops, right?

Yes, something *is* moving slowly between hops 9 and 10. It's called *light*. I'm in North America. The target web server is in Denmark. Hop 9 is on my continent, while hop 10 is on the other side of the Atlantic Ocean.

How do I know where the hosts are? There's no definitive thing that says that this target site is in Europe, but I can infer it from several clues. The most obvious hint is that the web site ends in `.dk`, the top level domain for Denmark. Checking who owned the domain names in hop hopes 11 and 12 would tell me that they belonged to a Danish ISP. If all else failed, I could identify the owner of those IP addresses.

A `traceroute` all the way around the Earth, at the equator, on good fiber, takes about 400 milliseconds.[22]

If you see a sudden time increase intermixed with asterisks, it can indicate problems starting at the first troubled router. Or it might be asymmetric routing, discussed below.

Multiple Hosts at One Hop

Sometimes you'll get multiple hostnames at one hop. Each hostname gets one or more timestamps.

Networks can load balance traffic just as servers can. A busy connection might have multiple routers. Each will return its own

---

22   On bad fiber, a trip around the world can take forever.

`traceroute` timestamp to the client. Traceroutes through highly redundant networks can show confusing tangles of routers. If you get this sort of issue, either spend the time to sort out exactly where each packet is going or ask a network engineer for his experienced assistance.

! Errors

Rather than a hostname or timestamp, sometimes a `traceroute` ends in an error code like !H or !X. These are specific `traceroute` errors indicating that the trace ends here. I'm not going to list all of the possible errors, but here are a few common ones.

A !H means that the next host is unreachable. The path is broken. You can't get there from here. Bridge Out.

Similarly, the !N error means that the entire destination network is unreachable.

A !A, !X, or !Z means that further communication is administratively prohibited. Someone has configured a packet filter to answer traceroutes with "None shall pass."

Identifying Address and Domain Owners

When you see something weird on a `traceroute`, you might well want to know who is responsible for those addresses or hosts. Use the *whois* service for this. You can find a lot of web-based whois services, or most Unix-like systems have a `whois` command.

You can ask whois about a domain or an IP address, and it will give you the registered contact or owner of that resource. All the information you provide to register a domain is available via whois, and IP address owners must provide similar contact information. While this isn't completely reliable, it usually gives you a clue as to the geographic location of a network.

Asymmetric Routing and Traceroute Servers

Each router makes its own independent decisions about how to route traffic. Large ISPs might have a common policy across all their routers, and those routers might share a common set of routing decisions. While each network presents certain routing information to the world, they can each make their own decisions about how to send traffic.

The route your packets take to reach a host might be different than the route that packets from that host take to reach you. While `traceroute` displays each hop along the way to a remote host, it doesn't display the return path. Every host along the way might take a totally different return path. On a fourteen-hop `traceroute`, most of the traffic might come straight back, but hop 12's response might pass through Uruguay and Norway due to that device's routing design. This is another reason to disregard high round trip times at a single hop.

While the myriad networks of the Internet all exchange routing information, not all networks show the same information to every other network. It's entirely possible that a network can send all of its traffic to Verizon via Poland, while routing AT&T through British Columbia. Why would they do this? Either they've made a mistake, or they really have no better alternative.

The resulting mishmash of paths is called *asymmetric routing*. It's simultaneously a key part of how the Internet works, and a curse to troubleshooting.

Suppose you have a `traceroute` that stars out at hop 9. Packets flowed just fine to routers 1 through 8, but your client gets nothing back from hop 9. If router 8 couldn't send traffic to router 9 you'd get a !H or a !N. Either hop 9 has filtering, or perhaps it sends packets back to you via a completely different route than that used for you to get there. That return path might be broken.

How can you tell which is which? If possible, have the client run a `traceroute` back to your servers. Compare both results.

What if the client can't do `traceroute`? That's where `traceroute` servers come in. Many sites let the public run `traceroute` from one of their machines. If your site can't reach a destination, see if other people can reach it. The web site traceroute. org lists hundreds of public `traceroute` servers. Retry your traceroutes from a site who uses the same carrier where your problem `traceroute` died. If you can't see an obvious issue in one traceroute, try several and compare the results.

Ongoing Traceroute: mtr

Every router drops a few packets now and then. How can you separate a rare loss from an ongoing problem?

By running more traceroutes!

Yes, you could just keep hitting the up arrow and ENTER, but that's tedious. If you want to watch network routes on an ongoing basis, I recommend `mtr` (for "my trace route,") available as a package on all operating systems. There's a Windows version, called WinMTR. Mtr runs `traceroute` continuously and prints packet and timing statistics.

How Should You Use Traceroute?

Given all the potential errors, how should you use or interpret `traceroute`?

Traceroutes of problems are most useful when compared to traceroutes of working connections. Become familiar with what things should look like, so you can recognize problems when they happen.

Compared to the global Internet, corporate networks are pretty simple. If a user in Farawayistan complains that they can't access your server, `traceroute` from the server to the client. If there's no layer 3 problem, you should be able to at least reach their site.

If you're having trouble reaching an Internet site, `traceroute` can offer insight into external network conditions. It can at least tell you that traffic has left your network—or, alternately, that everything's dying at your organization's Internet border. The network team probably already knows, but it might be time to poke your head over the top of your cubicle and ask.

If you really want to know more about `traceroute`, I highly recommend Richard A Steenbergen's presentation from NANOG 47, called "A Practical Guide to (Correctly) Troubleshooting with Traceroute." When I discovered this slide set, I crossed *Traceroute Mastery* off my to-do list.

`Traceroute` rounds out our discussion of network tools for sysadmins. Combined with an understanding of basic TCP/IP, you are now better equipped to solve problems than most of your peers. Congratulations!

Afterword

This is the part of the book where I admit that I've misled you.

No, not "lied!" Sheesh. *Misled.*

Yes, this book is about network protocols, and it's aimed at systems administrators. By reading this book and practicing with the tools therein, you've made yourself a better sysadmin. But really, this book is about changing your interactions with other IT teams within an organization.

I've been in more than one organization where the various groups within IT feel very frustrated with each other. Conflicting priorities and overly rigid or excessively porous boundaries lead to conflict, which causes bad feelings or, worse, lots and lots of meetings where everything gets painfully negotiated and still more processes get piled on everyone until absolutely all progress chokes on ceaseless paperwork.

Who's responsible for fixing or, better still, preventing this mess?

You are.

So is your coworker.

So is the person you've sworn an unbreakable blood oath of eternal vengeance against.

Afterword

Managers cannot improve interpersonal reactions. Managers can impose formal structure, and bad management can make things even worse, but even a good manager can't make two clashing personalities work together without imposing lots of formality.

But if an argument just keeps looping over and over the same ground, it's time to change the rules.

The quickest way to change a person's reactions to you is by earning their respect. The quickest way to earn an IT person's respect is to demonstrate intelligence and competence. Understanding the basics of TCP/IP lets you communicate more easily with the networking and security teams in your organization.

But someone has to start the change. It might as well be you. No, you can't single-handedly change your organization's culture. But you can control your interactions with other people. And a decent manager notices who improves the environment, and who tanks morale like an ACME anvil on a hungry coyote.

Even if you fail utterly, at least you'll finally know if that firewall port is open or not.

Never miss a new Lucas release!

Sign up for Michael W Lucas' mailing list.
https://mwl.io

More Tech Books from Michael W Lucas

Absolute BSD
Absolute OpenBSD (1st and 2nd edition)
Cisco Routers for the Desperate (1st and 2nd edition)
PGP and GPG
Absolute FreeBSD
Network Flow Analysis
Absolute FreeBSD 3rd edition

the IT Mastery Series

SSH Mastery (1st and 2nd edition)
DNSSEC Mastery
Sudo Mastery (1st and 2nd edition)
FreeBSD Mastery: Storage Essentials
Networking for Systems Administrators
Tarsnap Mastery
FreeBSD Mastery: ZFS
FreeBSD Mastery: Specialty Filesystems
FreeBSD Mastery: Advanced ZFS
PAM Mastery
Relayd and Httpd Mastery
Ed Mastery
FreeBSD Mastery: Jails

Novels (as Michael Warren Lucas)

git commit murder
Immortal Clay
Kipuka Blues
Butterfly Stomp Waltz
Terrapin Sky Tango
Hydrogen Sleets

182